S0-ACX-815

PACIFIC
LINERS
1927-72

By the same author, and uniform with this book

The Atlantic Liners 1925-70

PACIFIC LINERS 1927-72

FREDERICK EMMONS

ARCO PUBLISHING COMPANY, INC
New York

Published 1974 by
Arco Publishing Company, Inc.
219 Park Avenue South,
New York, N.Y. 10003

© 1973 by Frederick Emmons

All rights reserved

Library of Congress Catalog Card Number 73-86484
ISBN 0-668-03380-0

Printed in Great Britain

CONTENTS

SHIPS NOT ILLUSTRATED

FOREWORD

The development of the Pacific passenger liners was shaped by conditions far different from those which prevailed in the North Atlantic. The first was of course the sheer size of the ocean area with its sixty-eight million square miles of water, and its remoteness from the centres of world power and trade. Its shores to a large extent were sparsely settled by peoples whose civilisations by maritime standards at least, had not reached a stage of material development comparable to that of western Europe. Although the Polynesians, sailing by the stars in their double canoes, made voyages across thousands of miles of empty ocean at a time when the mariners of the Mediterranean rarely ventured out of sight of land, the establishment of overseas trade routes awaited the coming of European ships and sailors.

The demand for spices and the riches of the East led the navigators of fifteenth-century Europe to search for a way to the Indies by sailing along the coast of Africa and around the Cape, and Columbus finally sailed westward across the uncharted seas of the Atlantic in the hope of finding a shorter passage. It was left to Magellan's circumnavigating voyage of 1520, however, to link the newly discovered world of the Americas with the old world of Cathay. Within fifty years fleets of Spanish galleons, laden with treasure, were sailing homeward from the Philippines to the Isthmus of Panama.

In 1642 a Dutchman, Abel Tasman, made voyages of discovery to Tasmania, New Zealand, Fiji and Tonga, but it was not until late in the next century that the full expanse of the Pacific area was thoroughly explored by the most famous of contemporary navigators, Captain James Cook. His three great voyages up to the time of his death at the hands of Hawaiian natives in 1779, led to the modern mapping of the world.

The explorers were followed in the usual order by the traders and the colonizers. The first ships began to arrive in the empty land of Australia, and after 1830 immigration increased to reach a total of nearly 200,000 colonists over the next twenty years. The discovery of gold in California in 1848, and in Australia three years later, resulted in a rush of prospectors to the Pacific area and a subsequent increase in its maritime importance. A few years later Commodore Perry's 'black ships' opened the Japanese Shogunate to western trade.

By mid-century Australia and New Zealand had become self-governing colonies which continued to attract a steady flow of European immigrants. The development of agriculture led eventually to the export of frozen meat, wheat and wool which were to become mainstays of the overseas trade, and with the population concentrated in coastal cities, a flourishing network of intercolonial and coastal shipping services was established.

All this seafaring activity was on a very modest scale when compared to the floods of emigrants crossing the North Atlantic and the immense volume of commercial trade between Europe and America. Ships were small, voyages long, and the Lines were often dependent on mail subsidies for existence. Little of it involved the crossing of the Pacific except for the ships of the New Zealand Shipping Co and Shaw Savill which sailed home eastward through the 'roaring forties' by way of Cape Horn.

The first regular transpacific passenger service was established by the Pacific Mail Steamship Co with the sailing of the side-wheeler COLORADO from San Francisco in 1867. With the completion of the transcontinental railroads in the United States and Canada in the next few years, the transpacific steamship services became important as an extension of the route from the Orient to the population centres of the East Coast. Thus the Canadian Pacific sailed from Vancouver to become a competitor in the raw silk trade, and a few years later the N.Y.K. Line inaugurated a service to the terminus of the Great Northern Railroad at Seattle, then a city of 6,000 people.

The opening of the Panama Canal in 1914 shaped new routes of Pacific shipping. It shortened the distance from Europe to New Zealand, Tahiti and New Caledonia by over a thousand miles and became a factor in the development of the considerable Japanese emigrant trade to Brazil.

World War I affected Pacific shipping only to a limited degree and comparatively few ships were sunk by enemy action. The Japanese shipping services expanded enormously while the British and Americans were preoccupied with the struggle in the Atlantic, and the ships on the New Zealand trade were requisitioned to maintain the vital deliveries of frozen meat. One of the after effects was the advent in the early 1920s of new American competition in the Pacific when the Dollar Line and American Mail Line inaugurated new services with government-built vessels completed too late to participate in the war effort.

World War II, in contrast, was devasting in its effect. The tide of Japanese conquest engulfed the islands of the Dutch East Indies and lapped nearly to the shores of Australia, and two of the world's mightiest navies fought for four years from the Coral Sea to the Aleutians. In the end, Japan's merchant shipping was almost completely destroyed, while the American ships taken for war duty, though physically intact, returned to a different world. While the fighting was going on, the air age had arrived, and the fine new passenger ships converted to the uses of war were, with few exceptions, laid up at its end.

After the war the demand for emigrant passage from Europe to the underpopulated lands of Australia and New Zealand caused a temporary increase in passenger shipping on this route, and in 1954 the P & O Line ships inaugurated the extension of their sailings across the Pacific. With the closure of the Suez Canal in 1966 the ships on the Australian service were forced to sail via the Cape and an increasing number of voyages were made homeward on the shorter route across the Pacific. Thus, although the northern services of the Canadian Pacific and the Japanese lines did not survive the war, the Pacific area in general has retained a large number of regularly scheduled ships in contrast to the steady decline of Atlantic shipping with its massive air competition and limited tourist season. Of the twenty largest ships in the Pacific service, sixteen are currently in operation, and the only American-flag passenger ships still in service sail out of San Francisco.

It is evident however, that many of these ships will soon reach the end of their useful lives, and regular transpacific services will inevitably be drastically curtailed. Indeed, the scheduled withdrawal of a number of vessels has already been announced. The future of Pacific passenger shipping undoubtedly lies in the cruise liners which, in 1972, are beginning to appear in increasing numbers in this relatively uncrowded tourist area. With new ships designed for the service and conveniently based, the long voyages between distant ports are being eliminated by connecting flights from the major cities, and passenger ships are once again evolving to meet the changing needs of the times.

Frederick Emmons

EXPLANATORY NOTES

The passenger liners in the Pacific in 1927 included practically all the ships built for these services since the turn of the century. World War I, potentially the chief source of attrition, affected the Pacific ships to a very limited degree. Of the major shipping lines, three of the best known, Pacific Mail, Oceanic Steamship Co and Toyo Yusen Kaisha, had recently been absorbed by the Dollar Line, Matson Line and Nippon Yusen Kaisha respectively. Their ships are listed under the names of their new owners.

Listed are all the ships sailing since that time on the various transpacific services, as well as those on the Australia-New Zealand intercolonial and interstate trades. In limiting the scope to regularly scheduled Pacific shipping, the following are omitted:

1 Ships and lines serving Australia, New Zealand and the Far East from Europe via Suez or the Cape.
2 Ships on coastal services to Pacific ports of North and South America and the Asiatic mainland.
3 Atlantic liners sailing on off-season round-the-world or Pacific cruises.

The following information is recorded on each ship to the extent known:

1 Year built.
2 Years on Pacific service.
3 Gross registered tonnage.
4 Overall length and breadth in feet. (R) where noted, indicates registered length as listed in Lloyd's Register of Shipping until 1955 (roughly 20 feet less than overall length).
5 Number of screws, type of engines, service speed.
6 Name and location of builder.
7 Ports of departure and arrival, date of maiden voyage (M.V.), or first voyage (F.V.) on route.
8 Changes of owner and name.
9 War service.
10 Date and place of sinking or breaking up

Drawings are at a scale of 1 inch equals 160 feet.

ACKNOWLEDGEMENTS

The kind assistance of the following people, whose help provided much otherwise unavailable information on the various ships, is deeply appreciated: Mr Stephen Kentwell, Canberra, Australia; Mr W.G. MacDonald, formerly of American President Lines; the late Mr Albert Harmon, Librarian, San Francisco Maritime Museum; Mr Richard F. Zink, Orient Overseas Line; Mr Dudley Thickens, West Coast Branch, World Ship Society; Prof John Kemble, Pomona College; Mr D.W. Finch, Secretary, New South Wales Branch, World Ship Society; Mr D. Ridley Chesterton, Coulsdon, Surrey; Mr John B. Loan, Adelaide Steamship Co; Mr Fred A. Stindt, Matson Navigation Co; Mr Hishashi Noma, Mitsui-O.S.K. Lines, Tokyo and Mr Yoshitatsu Fukawa, Hiratsuka, Japan.

In addition, valuable data was received from the following organisations: Les Amis des Sept Mers, Paris; Burns, Philp & Co, China Navigation Co, P & O Lines, H.C. Sleigh Ltd, Royal Interocean Lines, Shaw Savill Line and Union Steam Ship Co of New Zealand.

1 GREAT BRITAIN

NEW ZEALAND SHIPPING CO, LONDON (1883-1969)

The New Zealand Shipping Co was formed at Christchurch in 1872 to operate a fleet of sailing vessels between the colony and the United Kingdom. As a requisite to obtaining a government mail contract, the first steamer voyage from London was made by the chartered BRITISH KING on 20 January 1883.

After 1884 the Line alternated with the Shaw Savill Line to provide fortnightly sailings via the Cape of Good Hope. Normal passage time was forty-five days outbound and forty-two days homeward bound around the Horn. The opening of the Panama Canal in 1914 reduced the length of the voyage by over 1000 miles, and after 1916 the Canal route was used in both directions. In that year the Company became a member of the P & O Group.

After World War II the fleet was modernised by the construction of three new ships, the RANGITOTO, RANGITANI and RUAHINE. The pre-war RANGITIKI and RANGITATA were disposed of in 1962 and replaced by the purchase of the Cunard liner PARTHIA which was refitted and renamed REMUERA only to be withdrawn from the service and transferred two years later.

In the late sixties, the increasing cost of operation plus air competition forced the Company to sell the three remaining ships and end a passenger service which had been maintained unbroken for 86 years.

1 RIMUTAKA
'00, (1901-29) 7,765. 457 (R) x 58. Twin screw, triple-expansion engines, 14 knots. Built by Wm Denny & Bros; Dumbarton. M.V. London-Capetown, Auckland and Wellington, 3 January 1901. Shifted to homeward route via Panama Canal 1915; to both ways after July 1916. Continued service under Government control throughout World War I. Refitted and resumed regular passenger service December 1920. Withdrawn from service December 1929; broken up Pembroke 1930.

2 RUAPEHU
'01, (1902-31) 7,705. Details as (1). Built by Wm Denny & Bros. Chartered by Allan Line (Great Britain) for Canadian service upon completion; temporarily renamed AUSTRALASIAN. Renamed RUAPEHU six months later. F.V. London-New Zealand via Capetown, 5 December 1901. Under Government control in World War I; resumed regular passenger service January 1921. Laid up at Falmouth, April 1931; broken up Savona, Italy.

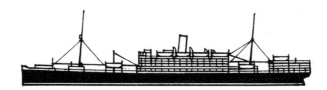

3 RUAHINE
'09, (1910-38) 10,839. 496 x 60. Twin screw, triple-expansion engines, 14 knots. Built by Wm Denny & Bros. M.V. London-New Zealand via Capetown, 28 November 1909; homeward voyage via Cape Horn. Changed to Panama Canal route 1916 while under war-time Government control. Refitted and converted to oil-burning 1920; resumed regular passenger service 2 December 1920. Laid up at Falmouth 1938. Due to war-time shipping shortage returned to New Zealand trade on cargo service under Government control 1939. Served as troopship 1940-1. Sold to Fratelli Grimaldi (Italy) after 91 New Zealand voyages 1949; renamed AURIGA and placed in Italy-Central America service. Broken up Savona 1957.

4 REMUERA

'11, (1911-40) 11,158. 501 x 62. Details as (3). Built by Wm Denny & Bros. M.V. London-New Zealand via Capetown, 28 September 1911. Changed to Panama Canal route August 1914, the first British ship to make the transit. Extensively refitted and converted to oil-burning 1920; resumed regular passenger service March 1921. Continued in New Zealand trade under Government control again in World War II to make use of large refrigerated cargo capacity. Sunk by torpedo bombers off Kinnaird's Head, Scotland, 26 August 1940.

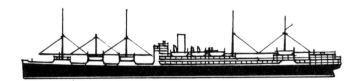

5 ROTORUA

'11, (1923-40) 12,112. 544 x 61. Twin screw, quadruple-expansion engines, 14 knots. Built by John Brown & Co; Clydebank, Glasgow as SHROPSHIRE for Federal Steam Navigation Co (Great Britain). M.V. Liverpool-Australia via Capetown, 28 October 1911. Served as troopship 1914-17. Laid up at Falmouth after damage by fire 1922. Transferred to New Zealand Shipping Co; converted to oil-burning and extensively refitted; renamed ROTORUA. F.V. Southampton-Auckland, Wellington, 29 March 1923. Torpedoed and sunk north of Scotland, 11 December 1940.

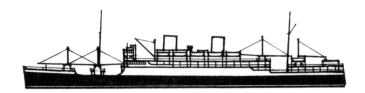

6 RANGITIKI

'29, (1929-62) 16,985. 552 x 70. Twin screw, motorship, 16 knots. Built by John Brown & Co; Clydebank, Glasgow. M.V. Southampton-Auckland, Wellington, 15 February 1929. Converted to troopship 1940. Re-engined and reconditioned 1948; resumed passenger service September 1948. Broken up Santander 1962.

7 RANGITATA

'29, (1929-62) 16,969. Details as (6). Built by John Brown & Co M.V. Southampton-New Zealand, 22 November 1929. Converted to troopship 1941. Re-engined and reconditioned; resumed passenger service September 1949. Sold to Dutch shipbreakers after 144 Panama Canal passages, May 1962; renamed RANG. Resold for breaking up at Split, Yugoslavia.

8 RANGITANE

'29, (1929-40) 16, 712. Details as (6). Built by John Brown & Co. M.V. Southampton-New Zealand, 20 December 1929. Captured and scuttled by German raiders ORION and KOMET in South Pacific on voyage from Auckland to United Kingdom, 27 November 1940.

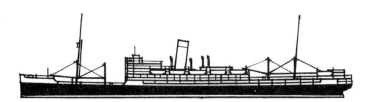

9 RIMUTAKA

'23, (1938-50) 15,043. 573 x 72. Twin screw, turbines, 15 knots. Built by Sir W.G. Armstrong-Whitworth & Co, Newcastle, as MONGOLIA for P & O Lines. Transferred to New Zealand Shipping Co as replacement for RUAHINE 1938. Sold to Incres Line (Panama) for transatlantic service February 1950; renamed EUROPA. Transferred to New York-Nassau service 1951; renamed NASSAU and registered in Liberia. Sold to Cia Naviera Turistica Mexicana (Mexico) 1961; renamed ACAPULCO. Laid up at Manzanillo, Mexico, May 1963; towed to Japan and broken up Osaka 1964.

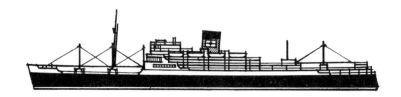

10 RANGITOTO

'49, (1949-69) 21,809. 609 x 78. Twin screw, motorship, 16.5 knots. Built by Vickers-Armstrongs, Newcastle. M.V. London-New Zealand, 25 August 1949. Sold to Orient Overseas Line 1969; renamed ORIENTAL CARNAVAL (225).

11 RANGITANE

'49, (1950-68) 21,867. Details as (10). Built by John Brown & Co. M.V. London-New Zealand, 27 January 1950. Sold to Astroguardia Cia Nav (Greece) for breaking up 1968; renamed JAN. Resold to Orient Overseas Line 1968; renamed ORIENTAL ESMERALDA (224).

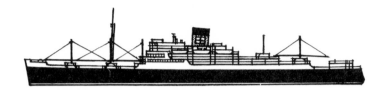

12 RUAHINE
'51, (1951-68) 17, 851. 585 x 75. Twin screw, motorship, 17 knots. Built by John Brown & Co, Clydebank, Glasgow. M.V. London-Auckland, Wellington, 22 May 1951. Sold to Orient Overseas Line 1968; renamed ORIENTAL RIO (223).

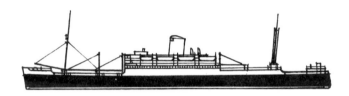

13 REMUERA
'48, (1962-4) 13,619. 534 x 70. Twin screw, turbines, 17 knots. Built by Harland & Wolff, Belfast as PARTHIA for Cunard Line (Great Britain). M.V. Liverpool-New York, 10 April 1948. Bought by New Zealand Shipping Co 1961; renamed REMUERA and refitted with increased passenger accommodation at Glasgow. F.V. London-New Zealand, 1 June 1962. Transferred to Eastern & Australian Steamship Co 1964; renamed ARAMAC (53).

SHAW SAVILL LINE, LONDON (1884-   )

In 1858 Robert Shaw and Walter Savill established a company in opposition to the Albion Line of Glasgow which operated a fleet of sailing ships carrying emigrants between Britain and New Zealand.

The two companies were joined in 1882 to form Shaw, Savill & Albion Co to which Shaw Savill contributed twenty-six vessels and Albion twelve. In coordination with the New Zealand Shipping Co a monthly mail and passenger service was begun with the sailing of the steamer ARAWA from London on 5 November 1884. Three of the original five steamers on the service were surplus ships owned by the White Star Line and were operated on a profit-sharing basis. Outward voyages were made by way of the Cape of Good Hope, returning via Cape Horn and the east coast of South America, but after 1916 the shorter Panama Canal route was used in both directions.

After World War II a quartet of passenger-cargo liners was built,.and in 1955 the revolutionary engines-aft SOUTHERN CROSS was commissioned. She was placed on a regular round-the-world service, making two voyages in each direction per year. A running mate, the NORTHERN STAR, joined her seven years later.

In 1968 the Line purchased three Royal Mail ships, the AMAZON, ARLANZA and ARAGON, which were renamed AKAROA, ARAWA and ARANDA and placed on the round-the-world service. However, in 1971 they were sold for conversion to car carriers, while the SOUTHERN CROSS was laid up at the end of the year. The service was continued by the OCEAN MONARCH, the former Canadian Pacific liner EMPRESS OF ENGLAND.

14 ATHENIC
'01, (1902-28) 12,234. 530 x 63. Twin screw, quadruple expansion engines, 14 knots. Built by
Harland & Wolff, Belfast for White Star Line (Great Britain); managed by Shaw Savill for joint
New Zealand service. M.V. London-Teneriffe, Capetown, Hobart and Wellington, 13 February
1902. Homeward voyage via Montevideo and Rio de Janeiro. Served as troopship 1914-15;
requisitioned by British Government for shipping frozen meat during remaining war years.
Routed through Panama Canal after 1916. Resumed regular passenger service January 1920. Sold
to Hvalfangersk Pelagos A/S (Norway) for conversion to whale factory ship 1928; renamed
PELAGOS. Broken up Hamburg 1962.

15 CORINTHIC
'02, (1902-31) 12,231. Details as (14). Built by Harland & Wolff for White Star Line. M.V. London-
Wellington, 12 November 1902. Requisitioned during war; resumed regular passenger service January
1920. Broken up Blyth 1931.

16 IONIC
'02, (1903-36) 12,232. Details as (14). Built by Harland & Wolff for White Star Line. M.V. London-
Wellington, 16 January 1903. Requisitioned during war; resumed passenger service January 1919.
Transferred to Shaw Savill Line 1934. Broken up Japan 1937.

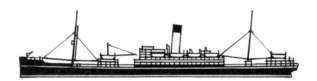

17 ARAWA
'07, (1907-28) 9,372. 480 x 60. Twin screw, triple expansion engines, 13.5 knots. Built by Swan,
Hunter & Wigham Richardson, Wallsend-on-Tyne. M.V. London-Wellington, 22 August 1907.
Served as troopship 1914-15; requisitioned by British Government during remaining war years.
Resumed regular passenger service May 1921. Sold to Arnold Bernstein (Germany) 1928; renamed
KONIGSTEIN and operated as cargo ship. Passenger accommodation reinstalled 1931. Sold to
shipbreakers at Ghent 1939. Due to wartime shipping shortage, reconverted to cargo ship; renamed
GANDIA. Chartered to Cie Maritime Belge (Belgium) December 1939. Torpedoed and sunk in
North Atlantic with loss of 65 lives, 22 January 1942.

18 TAINUI

'08, (1908-39) 9,957. 499 x 61. Twin screw, triple expansion engines, 14 knots. Built by Workman, Clark & Co, Belfast. M.V. London-New Zealand via Suez, 12 November 1908. Requisitioned during war; torpedoed April 1918 and abandoned in English Channel but reboarded and towed in sinking condition 130 miles to Falmouth. Resumed regular passenger service September 1921. Sold to shipbreakers 1939 but bought by Ministry of War Transport; renamed EMPIRE TRADER. Torpedoed and sunk in mid-Atlantic, 21 February 1943.

19 TAMAROA

'22, (1926-57) 12,361. 519 x 63. Twin screw, turbines, 15 knots. Built by Harland & Wolff, Belfast as SOPHOCLES for Aberdeen Line (Great Britain). M.V. London-Capetown, Sydney and Brisbane, 1 March 1922. Chartered by Shaw Savill Line for service to New Zealand via Panama Canal 1926; renamed TAMAROA. Served as troopship 1940-7. Refitted at Liverpool; resumed passenger service August 1948. Broken up Blyth 1957.

20 MATAROA

'22, (1926-57) 12,341. Details as (19). Built by Harland & Wolff as DIOGENES for Aberdeen Line. M.V. London-Australia via the Cape, 16 August 1922. Chartered by Shaw Savill Line 1926; renamed MATAROA. Requisitioned as troopship, December 1940. Refitted at Glasgow 1947; resumed passenger service April 1948. Broken up Faslane 1957.

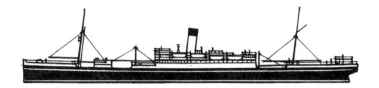

21 AKAROA
'14, (1932-54) 15,320. 570 x 67. Triple screw, triple-expansion engines and L.P. turbine, 15 knots. Built by Harland & Wolff as EURIPIDES for Aberdeen Line. M.V. London-Capetown, Sydney and Brisbane, 1 July 1914. Taken over as troopship upon arrival at Brisbane; resumed passenger service February 1919. Bought by Shaw Savill Line 1932; renamed AKAROA. Extensively remodelled on the Tyne; changed to oil-burning. F.V. Southampton-New Zealand, 30 December 1932. Served on New Zealand route throughout World War II. Broken up Antwerp 1954.

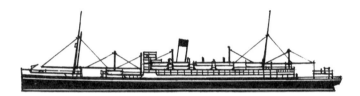

22 ARAWA
'22, (1937-47) 14,491. 549 x 68. Twin screw, turbines, 15 knots. Built by Wm. Beardmore & Co, Dalmuir as ESPERANCE BAY for Commonwealth Government Line (Australia). M.V. London-Australia via Suez, 1 August 1922. Transferred to Shaw Savill Line as replacement for IONIC September 1936; renamed ARAWA. Extensively refitted on the Clyde. F.V. Southampton-Wellington and westbound round-the-world, 22 January 1937. Commissioned as armed merchant cruiser October 1939; converted to troopship 1941. Resumed passenger service 1946. Shifted to London-Australia, New Zealand service via Capetown August 1947. Broken up Newport 1955.

23 WAIRANGI
'42, (1946-51) 13,478. 540 x 70. Twin screw, motorship, 16 knots. Built by Harland & Wolff as EMPIRE GRACE for Ministry of War Transport. Fitted with 112 tourist class berths as war-time measure. Bought by Shaw Savill Line 1946; renamed WAIRANGI. Passenger accommodation removed 1951. Stranded near Sandhamn, Sweden, 14 August 1963; refloated and towed to Faslane for breaking up.

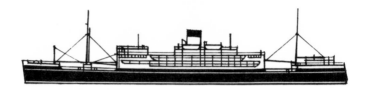

24 CORINTHIC
'47, (1947-65) 15,682. 560 x 71. Twin screw, turbines, 17 knots. 85 passengers. Built by Cammell Laird & Co, Birkenhead. M.V. Liverpool-Capetown, Sydney, 12 April 1947; subsequent voyages via Panama Canal. Passenger accommodation removed at Schiedam 1965. Broken up Kaohsiung 1969.

25 ATHENIC
'47, (1947-65) 15,187. Details as (24). Built by Harland & Wolff, Belfast. M.V. London-Auckland, 1 August 1947. Passenger accommodation removed on Tyne 1965. Broken up Kaohsiung 1969.

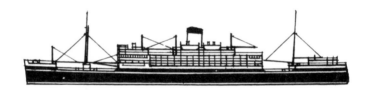

26 CERAMIC
'48, (1948-69) 15,896. 561 x 72. Twin screw, turbines, 17 knots. 85 passengers. Built by Cammell Laird & Co M.V. Liverpool-Auckland, 16 November 1948. Ceased carrying passengers 1969. Broken up Tamise, Belgium 1972.

27 GOTHIC
'48, (1948-68) 15,109. Details as (26). Built by Swan, Hunter & Wigham Richardson, Wallsend-on-Tyne. M.V. Liverpool-Sydney, 23 December 1948; subsequent voyages via Panama Canal. Commissioned as Royal Yacht to carry Queen Elizabeth II and Duke of Edinburgh on tour of Australasia 1952. Caught fire in South Pacific; bridge and superstructure gutted with loss of seven lives, 2 August 1968. Returned to Wellington for temporary repairs. Broken up Kaohsiung 1969.

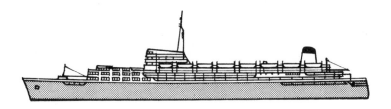

28 SOUTHERN CROSS
'55, (1955-71) 19,313. 604 x 79. Twin screw, motorship, 20 knots. Built by Harland & Wolff.
M.V. Southampton-round-the-world, 29 March 1955. Laid up at Southampton November 1971;
shifted to River Fal April 1972.

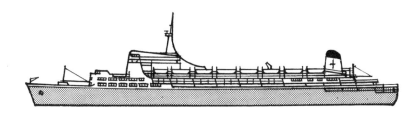

29 NORTHERN STAR
'62, (1962-   ) 23,983. 650 x 84. Twin screw, turbines, 19.5 knots. Built by Vickers-Armstrongs,
Walker-on-Tyne. M.V. Southampton-round-the-world, 10 July 1962.

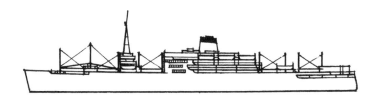

30 AKAROA
'59, (1968-71) 18,565. 584 x 78. Twin screw, motorship, 17 knots. Built by Harland & Wolff,
Belfast, as AMAZON for Royal Mail Lines (Great Britain). M.V. Southampton-Buenos Aires, 22
January 1960. Bought by Shaw Savill Line 1968; renamed AKAROA. F.V. London Australia, New
Zealand, 28 May 1968. Sold to A/S Uglands Rederi (Norway) 1971. Converted to car carrier at
Rijeka for Hoegh-Ugland Auto Liners; renamed AKARITA.

31 ARAWA
'60, (1969-71) 18,595. Details as (30). Built by Harland & Wolff as ARLANZA for Royal Mail Lines. Bought by Shaw Savill Line 1968; renamed ARAWA. F.V. London-Australia, New Zealand, 28 February 1969. Sold to Leif Hoegh & Co (Norway) 1971. Converted to car carrier at Rijeka; renamed HOEGH TRANSIT. Renamed HOEGH TROTTER during conversion.

32 ARANDA
'60, (1969-71) 18,575. Details as (30). Built by Harland & Wolff as ARAGON for Royal Mail Line. Bought by Shaw Savill Line 1968; renamed ARANDA. F.V. London-Australia, New Zealand, 28 March 1969. Sold to Leif Hoegh & Co 1971. Converted to car carrier at Rijeka; renamed HOEGH TRAVELLER.

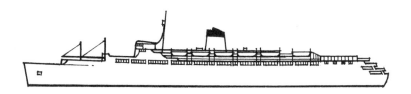

33 OCEAN MONARCH
'57, (1971-   ) 25,971. 640 x 85. Twin screw, turbines, 20 knots. Built by Vickers-Armstrongs, Walker-on-Tyne as EMPRESS OF ENGLAND for Canadian Pacific (Great Britain). M.V. Liverpool-Montreal, 18 April 1957. Bought by Shaw Savill Line February 1970; renamed OCEAN MONARCH. After one voyage to Australia, refitted as tourist class cruise ship at Birkenhead 1970-1. F.V. Southampton-Auckland, 5 November 1971.

CANADIAN PACIFIC, LONDON (1887-1941)

The Canadian Pacific Railway Co was incorporated in 1881 to build a railway across Canada. As part of the project an ocean link across the Pacific was envisioned as necessary to provide a flow of freight and passengers from the Orient.

In 1886, three weeks after the first train crossed the continent, a cargo of tea was delivered by a chartered sailing vessel to the temporary terminal at Port Moody, British Columbia and despatched by rail to eastern cities. In June of the following year, the steamer ABYSSINIA one of three under Company charter from the Guion Line, arrived in Vancouver with a shipment of silk to inaugurate the Company's ocean services. Three new ships were ordered in 1889, and the first of the trio, the EMPRESS OF INDIA made the first transpacific crossing from Hong Kong to Vancouver on 7 April 1891.

In 1913 two sister ships, the EMPRESS OF RUSSIA and EMPRESS OF ASIA joined the fleet but were soon requisitioned as armed merchant cruisers upon the outbreak of war. Soon after the end of hostilities the EMPRESS OF CANADA was placed in service, followed in 1928 by the luxurious EMPRESS OF JAPAN which made a record-breaking first crossing of the Pacific.

The four Pacific Empresses served as transports during World War II from which the EMPRESS OF JAPAN, by then renamed EMPRESS OF SCOTLAND, emerged as the sole survivor. The heavy losses suffered by the Line made it impossible to re-open the transpacific service, and the EMPRESS OF SCOTLAND was transferred to the Atlantic at the completion of her military duties.

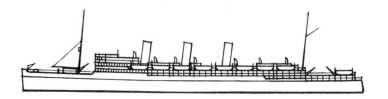

34   EMPRESS OF RUSSIA

'13, (1913-45) 16,810. 590 x 68. Quadruple screw, turbines, 19 knots. Built by Fairfield Ship-building & Engineering Co, Govan, Glasgow. M.V. Liverpool-Hong Kong, 1 April 1913. Commissioned as armed merchant cruiser for service in Indian Ocean, August 1914. Served as troopship in Atlantic 1918-19. Refitted at Hong Kong; resumed passenger service March 1919. Requisitioned once more as troopship after 310 transpacific crossings, November 1940. Gutted by fire at Barrow while refitting for passenger service, 8 September 1945; broken up the following year.

35   EMPRESS OF ASIA

'13, (1913-42) 16,908. Details as (34). Built by Fairfield S.B. & E. Co. M.V. Liverpool-Hong Kong, 14 June 1913. Commissioned as armed merchant cruiser August 1914. Served as troopship in Atlantic 1918-19. Resumed passenger service February 1919. In collision with, and sank freighter TUNG SHING near Shanghai, 11 January 1926. Converted to troopship February 1940. Sunk by Japanese planes off Singapore, 5 February 1942.

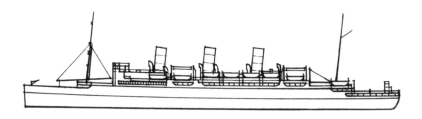

36   EMPRESS OF CANADA

'22, (1922-43) 21,516. 653 x 78. Twin screw, turbines, 19 knots. Built by Fairfield S.B. & E. Co. M.V. Falmouth-Hong Kong, 5 May 1922. Made first Canadian Pacific round-the-world cruise, leaving New York January 1924. Re-engined on the Clyde 1928-9; speed increased to 21 knots. Returned to trans-pacific service October 1929. Requisitioned as troopship November 1939. Torpedoed and sunk by Italian submarine in South Atlantic, 13 March 1943 while homeward bound from Durban with Italian prisoners of war.

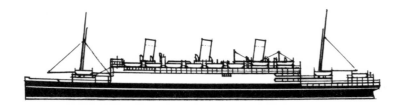

37   EMPRESS OF AUSTRALIA

'19, (1922-6) 21,860. 615 x 75. Twin screw, turbines, 17 knots. Launched 1913 by A.G. Vulkan Werke, Stettin as TIRPITZ for Hamburg American Line (Germany); work delayed by war. Allocated to British Government as war reparation 1919. Bought by Canadian Pacific 1921; renamed EMPRESS OF CHINA. Refitted at Hamburg; renamed EMPRESS OF AUSTRALIA 1922. Left Clyde on first voyage to Vancouver, 16 June 1922. Figured prominently in rescue and relief work at Yokohama during earthquake of 1 September 1923. Left Hong Kong for Atlantic, 4 August 1926 after 20 Pacific voyages. Re-engined at Glasgow 1926-7; returned to transatlantic service 25 June 1927 carrying Prince of Wales to Diamond Jubilee celebration of the Canadian Confederation. Converted to troopship, September 1939 and remained in trooping service until broken up Inverkeithing 1952.

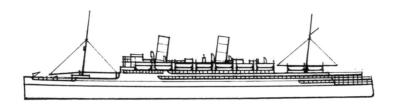

38   EMPRESS OF FRANCE

'13, (1928-9) 18,481. 600 x 72. Quadruple screw, turbines, 18 knots. Built by Wm Beardmore & Co, Glasgow as ALSATIAN for Allan Line (Great Britain). M.V. Liverpool-Halifax, 17 January 1914. Commissioned as armed merchant cruiser August 1914; served as flagship of Tenth Cruiser Squadron. Allan Line taken over by Canadian Pacific 1917. Refitted at Glasgow 1919; renamed EMPRESS OF FRANCE. F.V. Liverpool-Quebec, 26 September 1919. Converted to oil-burning 1924. Left Southampton for Pacific via Suez, 31 October 1928 as replacement for EMPRESS OF CANADA; returned to transatlantic service from Hong Kong, 17 October 1929. Laid up on the Clyde, September 1931; broken up Dalmuir 1934.

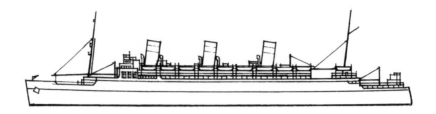

39 EMPRESS OF JAPAN

'30, (1930-9) 26,313. 666 x 84. Twin screw, turbines, 22 knots. Built by Fairfield Shipbuilding &
Engineering Co, Govan, Glasgow. Left Southampton for Hong Kong, 12 July 1930 after one trans-
atlantic voyage to Quebec. Broke transpacific speed record April 1931, crossing from Yokohama to
Vancouver in 7 days, 6 hours, 27 minutes. Converted to troopship, November 1939. Renamed
EMPRESS OF SCOTLAND 1942 after Japanese entry into war. Returned to passenger service on
Atlantic, May 1950. Sold to Hamburg Atlantic Lines (West Germany) January 1958; renamed
HANSEATIC. Extensively rebuilt; one funnel removed and tonnage increased to 30,030. Severely
damaged by fire at pier at New York, 7 September 1966. Towed to Hamburg for repairs but
broken up after survey revealed extent of damage.

ORIENT LINE, LONDON (1954-64)

In 1877 the London shipbroker firm of Anderson, Anderson & Co in conjunction with Frederick Green & Co, chartered four surplus steamers of the Pacific Steam Navigation Co to provide a passenger service to Australia via the Cape. The first of the quartet, the LUSITANIA, left Plymouth 28 June 1877. The sailings were successful, and the Orient Steam Navigation Co was formed the following year to purchase the four steamers and begin a monthly service from London.

A fleet was built up in conjunction with the Pacific S. N. Co, the first of which was the ORIENT of 1879, followed two years later by the AUSTRAL. After 1883 all regular sailings to Australia were made via Suez.

New vessels were continually added, and with the advent of the ORMUZ and Pacific S. N. Co's OROYA and ORIZABA, the 'O' names became standard. After 1901 the service was operated as the Orient-Pacific Line, but in 1906 the Pacific S. N. Co sold its Australian fleet to the Royal Mail Steam Packet Co and a new association was formed under the name of Orient-Royal Mail. This, in turn, was dissolved in 1909 and the four Royal Mail ships were withdrawn from the Australian trade. To meet the emergency, five new ships were built to provide a fleet capable of maintaining a fortnightly service.

All the Line's ships were taken for service in World War I, during which four were lost, and for a period after the war three ex-German ships were employed. Again in the Second World War, the entire fleet of eight ships was requisitioned, with but four survivors.

The first post-war ship, the ORCADES, was built in 1948, followed by the ORONSAY and ORSOVA. Shortly afterwards a transpacific service was begun with the voyage of the ORONSAY from Sydney to Vancouver and San Francisco January 1954.

In 1960 the Line's services were integrated with the P & O, as P & O-Orient Lines, and four years later the Orient Line ships lost their distinctive corn-coloured hulls in favour of the white P & O livery. In 1966 the name reverted to P & O Lines to mark the end of the Orient Line name after eighty-seven years of service.

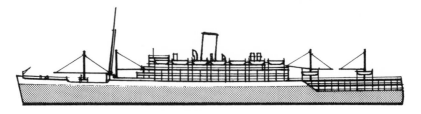

40 ORION·
'35, (1954-5) 23,696. 665 x 82. Twin screw, turbines, 19 knots. Built by Vickers-Armstrongs, Barrow-in-Furness. M.V. London-Melbourne, Sydney and Brisbane, 28 September 1935. Converted to transport September 1939. Damaged in collision with battleship **HMS REVENGE** September 1941. Refitted at Barrow 1946; resumed passenger service, 25 February 1947. Extended service across Pacific from Sydney, 17 September 1954; continued for three round voyages. Chartered for four months as hotel ship at Hamburg June 1964; broken up Tamise, Belgium.

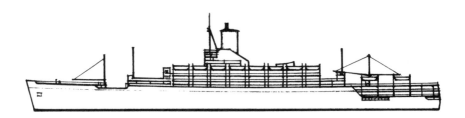

41 ORCADES
'48, (1955-72) 28,472. 709 x 94. Twin screw, turbines, 22 knots. Built by Vickers-Armstrongs. M.V. London-Fremantle, Melbourne and Sydney, 14 December 1948. Inaugurated westward transpacific route from London via Panama Canal to West Coast, New Zealand and Australia, August 1955. Transferred to P & O Lines 1964. Laid up at Southampton October 1972.

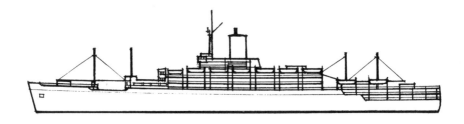

42 ORONSAY
'51, (1954-   ) 28,136. 709 x 90. Twin screw, turbines, 22 knots. Built by Vickers-Armstrongs. M.V. London-Fremantle, Melbourne and Sydney, 16 May 1951. Inaugurated extension of service from Sydney to Honolulu, Vancouver, San Francisco and Los Angeles, 1 January 1954. Transferred to P & O Lines 1964. To be withdrawn from service 1973.

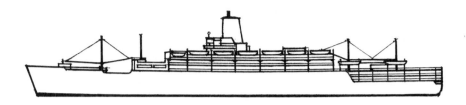

43 ORSOVA
'54, (1955-   ) 29,091 723 x 90. Twin screw, turbines, 22 knots. Built by Vickers-Armstrongs, Barrow-in-Furness. M.V. London-Melbourne, Sydney, 17 March 1954. Extended service across Pacific to West Coast, May 1955. Transferred to P & O Lines 1965.

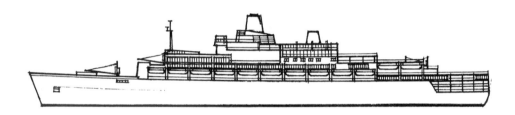

44 ORIANA
'60, (1961-   ) 41,910. 804 x 97. Twin screw, turbines, 27.5 knots. Built by Vickers-Armstrongs. M.V. Southampton-Melbourne, Sydney, San Francisco and Los Angeles. 3 December 1960. Returned to England via Sydney; round voyage completed in 111 days. Transferred to P & O Lines 1965.

C

P & O LINES, LONDON (1958-   )

The P & O, the largest, and one of the oldest and most famous of British shipping firms, is an outgrowth of the Peninsular Steam Navigation Co which operated in the coastal trade to Portugal and Spain. A mail contract was awarded in 1837, and when this was extended three years later to include Egypt, the Company was reorganised as the Peninsular & Oriental Steam Navigation Co. A service to India was begun in 1843, the passengers travelling overland from Alexandria to trans-ship at Suez.

The opening of the Suez Canal in November 1869 started a programme of building vessels capable of 'through' sailing. Over the years, the fleet expanded to the point where the Line was operating ten 'M' class steamers, starting with the MOLDAVIA of 1903, which were offering fortnightly sailings to Australia. By 1914 the ships on this service alone numbered sixteen. In May of that year the Company amalgamated with the British India Steam Navigation Co, the first step in the formation of the P & O Shipping Group which was to become the largest shipping combine in the world.

Passenger service was badly disrupted with heavy shipping losses during World War I, although reduced sailings were continued as necessary to maintain the mails. In the Second World War, however, all the available ships were requisitioned for trooping and the mails were carried by 'plane. Of the Line's nineteen passenger vessels, seven were lost.

After World War II, the first new construction for the Australia-New Zealand service was the HIMALAYA in 1949, followed by the ARCADIA and IBERIA, while the CHUSAN was built for the Far Eastern trade. The HIMALAYA entered the trans-pacific service in March 1958 when she left Sydney for Vancouver and San Francisco.

Services on the Pacific were integrated with the Orient Line in 1960 under the name P &O-Orient Lines, but in October 1966 the 'Orient' was dropped and ships of both companies have since sailed under the P & O Line's name and livery.

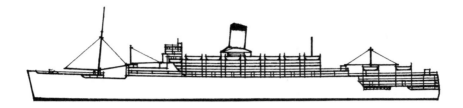

45   HIMALAYA
'49, (1958-   ) 28,047. 709 x 91. Twin screw, turbines, 22 knots. Built by Vickers-Armstrongs,
Barrow-in-Furness. M.V. London-Bombay, Colombo, Melbourne and Sydney, 6 October 1949.
Extended voyage from Sydney to Auckland, Vancouver and San Francisco, 21 March 1958.

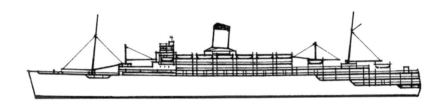

46   CHUSAN
'50, (1960-   ) 24,318. 673 x 85. Twin screw, turbines, 22 knots. Built by Vickers-Armstrongs.
Delivered June 1950. F.V. London-Bombay, 15 September 1950. Entered transpacific service 1960.
To be withdrawn from service March 1973.

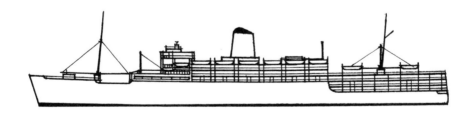

47   ARCADIA
'54, (1959-   ) 29,871. 721 x 91. Twin screw, turbines, 22 knots. Built by John Brown & Co,
Clydebank, Glasgow. M.V. London-India, Australia, 22 February 1954. Entered transpacific
service November 1959.

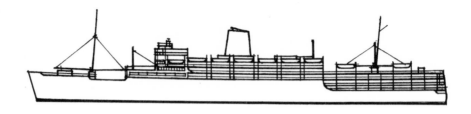

48   IBERIA

'54. (1960-72) 29,779. 719 x 91. Twin screw, turbines, 22 knots. Built by Harland & Wolff, Belfast. M.V. London-Bombay, Colombo, Melbourne and Sydney, 28 September 1954. Badly damaged in collision with tanker STANVAC PRETORIA off Colombo, 27 March 1956. Voyage extended to include transpacific service January 1960. Laid up at Southampton April 1972; broken up Kaohsiung.

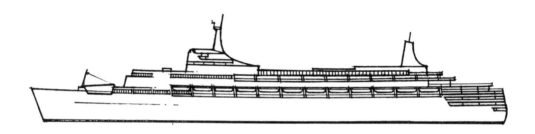

49   CANBERRA

'61, (1961-   ) 44,807. 818 x 103. Twin screw, turbo-electric, 27 knots. Built by Harland & Wolff; the largest British-built passenger ship since the QUEEN ELIZABETH of 1940. M.V. Southampton-Colombo, Melbourne, Sydney and transpacific, 2 June 1961. Disabled in Mediterranean by fire in main electrical switchboard, 5 January 1963; reached Malta under own power but forced to return to builders for repairs.

EASTERN & AUSTRALIAN STEAMSHIP CO, LONDON (1873-   )

The Eastern & Australian Steamship Co Ltd was formed in 1873 on the basis of a contract with the Queensland Government to carry mail between Singapore and Brisbane, later extended to Hong Kong and Melbourne. Four ships were chartered for the service, and the first sailing was made by the steamer SUNFOO from Singapore in November 1873. Unfortunately she stranded near Hong Kong on her return voyage early the following year. The route of this pioneer service lay from Hong Kong to Manila, Singapore, Batavia, Samarang and Sourabaya; through Torres Strait, then via Queensland ports to Brisbane, Sydney and Melbourne.

In 1881 control of the Company was taken by Anthony Gibbs & Sons, a London firm of merchant bankers. The first sizable vessel was the liner ST ALBANS of 1910, which was also the last new passenger ship to enter the Company's service. In 1920 the Line was sold by the Gibbs family to become a subsidiary of the British India Steam Navigation Co and thus a member of the P & O Group. From this time onward all the Company's passenger ships were transfers from other members of the Group.

The first addition was the ex-German liner SWAKOPMUND, requisitioned by the British Government as war reparation and renamed ARAFURA upon entering E & A service. The former British India liner TANDA was added in 1924, and in 1929-31 two additional British India ships, the NELLORE and NANKIN, were transferred as replacements for the ARAFURA and ST ALBANS which were sold for breaking up. All three were lost in World War II, leaving the Company without a passenger ship.

In 1965, however, the New Zealand Shipping Co's liner REMUERA was acquired and renamed ARAMAC to open an Australia-Japan service. She, in turn, was replaced by two P & O sisters, the CATHAY and CHITRAL, which were transferred in 1969-70 without change of name.

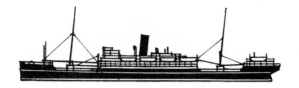

50 TANDA

'14, (1924-44) 6,956. 446 x 58. Twin screw, triple expansion engines, 14 knots. Built by Alexander Stephen & Sons, Linthouse, Glasgow for British India Steam Navigation Co (Great Britain). Chartered to Indian Government for conversion to hospital ship 1914; renamed MADRAS. Reverted to British India 1920; renamed TANDA. Transferred to Eastern & Australian Steamship Co 1924. Route: Australia-Manila, Hong Kong and Japan; shifted to Australia-India service after Japanese entry into World War II. Torpedoed and sunk off west coast of India near Mangalore, 15 July 1944.

51 NELLORE

'13, (1929-44) 6,942. 450 (R) x 52. Twin screw, quadruple expansion engines, 13 knots. Built as cargo ship by Caird & Co, Greenock for P & O Lines. Transferred to Eastern & Australian Steamship Co as replacement for ARAFURA (223) 1929; passenger accommodation added. Torpedoed and sunk in Indian Ocean, 29 June 1944.

52 NANKIN

'12, (1931-42) 6,069. Details as (51). Built by Caird & Co for P & O Lines. Transferred to Eastern & Australian Steamship Co as replacement for ST ALBANS (222) 1931. Captured by German raider THOR in South Indian Ocean, 10 May 1942. Sailed to Japan under prize crew; renamed LEUTHEN. Destroyed by fire along with THOR following explosion in tanker UCKERMARK during conversion to supply ship at Yokohama, 30 November 1942.

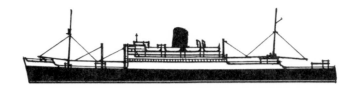

53 ARAMAC

'48, (1965-9) 13,619. Formerly REMUERA (13) New Zealand Shipping Co. Transferred to
Eastern & Australian Steamship Co 1964; renamed ARAMAC. F.V. Melbourne-Yokohama, 8
February 1965. Broken up Kaohsiung 1969.

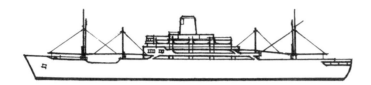

54 CATHAY

'57, (1969-) 13,809. 558 x 70. Twin screw, turbines, 16.5 knots. Built by S.A. Cockerill-Ougree,
Hoboken as BAUDOUINVILLE for Cie Maritime Belge (Belgium). Bought by P & O Lines 1961;
renamed CATHAY. F.V. Southampton-Japan, 14 April 1961. Transferred to Eastern & Australian
Steamship Co October 1969. F.V. Melbourne, Sydney, Brisbane-Yokohama, 13 December 1969.

55 CHITRAL

'56, (1970-) 13,821. Details as (54). Built by S.A. Chantiers et Ateliers de St. Nazaire (Penhoet)
as JADOTVILLE for Cie Maritime Belge. Bought by P & O Lines 1961; renamed CHITRAL. F.V.
Southampton-Japan, 2 March 1961. Transferred to Eastern & Australian Steamship Co September
1970. F.V. Australia-Japan, November 1970.

CHINA NAVIGATION CO, LONDON (1881-   )

In 1866 John Samuel Swire, together with friends interested in the China trade, formed a Shanghai branch of the fifty year old firm of John Swire & Sons under the name of Butterfield & Swire. Six years later the affiliated China Navigation Co was formed to run British steamers on the Yangtze River under their management. The Company's activities soon expanded to include most of the China coastal and river trade, and in 1881 a service to Australia was established. By 1941 the fleet had grown to fifty-seven ships totalling over 150,000 gross tons to make it the largest British shipping company operating solely in the Far East.

The Japanese occupation of Shanghai badly disrupted Chinese trade and World War II took a serious toll of the fleet. The Company's services were further reduced by the Anglo-Chinese treaty of 1943 which reserved the Chinese river and coastal trade for Chinese vessels. However, a post-war building programme was begun, and in 1949 the passenger ships CHANGSHA and TAIYUAN were delivered, followed by the ANKING and ANSHUN the following year.

The British troopship DILWARA was purchased in 1960, renamed KUALA LUMPUR, and converted to a dual purpose vessel for cruising and pilgrim services to the Red Sea. Three of the four passenger ships were sold between 1969 and 1971, and during the same period the Lloyd Brasiliero liner PRINCESA LEOPOLDINA was acquired and refitted as the cruise ship CORÁL PRINCESS.

56 CHANGSHA
'49, (1949-69) 7,412. 440 x 57. Single screw, motorship, 15 knots. 84 passengers. Built by Scott's Shipbuilding & Engineering Co, Greenock. Delivered May 1949. F.V. Australia-Japan, July 1949. Route: Melbourne, Sydney, Brisbane-Manila, Hong Kong and Yokohama. Sold to Pacific International Lines (Singapore) June 1969; renamed KOTA PANJANG.

57 TAIYUAN
'49, (1950-72) 6,160. Details as (56). Built by Scott's S B & E Co. Delivered November 1949. F.V. Australia-Japan, February 1950. Transferred to Sydney, Brisbane-Noumea, Suva service, July 1971. Sold to Pacific International Lines 1972; renamed KOTA SAHABAT.

58 ANKING
'50, (1950-70) 5,450. 418 x 57. Single screw, motorship, 14.5 knots. 50 passengers. Built by Scott's S B & E Co. Delivered January 1950. Route: Hong Kong-Keelung. Sold to Straits Steamship Co (Singapore) May 1970; renamed KLIAS.

59 ANSHUN
'50, (1951-68) 5,578. Details as (58). Built by Taikoo Dockyard & Engineering Co, Hong Kong. Delivered December 1950. For a number of years operated in the pilgrim trade from Singapore and Malaya to Jeddah for six months of the year. Sold to Pan-Islamic Steamship Co (Pakistan) 1971; renamed SAFINA-E-ABID.

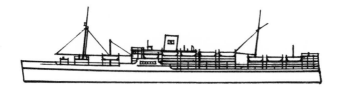

60   KUALA LUMPUR
'35, (1960-71) 12,555. 517 x 63. Twin screw, motorship, 14 knots. Built by Barclay, Curle & Co, Glasgow as troopship DILWARA for British India Steam Navigation Co (Great Britain). Delivered January 1936. Served throughout war; refitted to post-war trooping standards 1949. Bought by China Navigation Co November 1960; renamed KUALA LUMPUR. Refitted at Hong Kong for dual role as pilgrim ship and cruise liner. Route: Pilgrim voyages to Jeddah from Singapore, Port Swettenham and Penang, November to June; cruising from Australia and New Zealand in off season. Broken up Kaohsiung 1971.

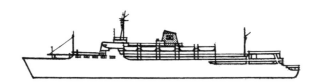

61   CORAL PRINCESS
'62, (1971-   ) 9,639. 478 x 61. Twin screw, motor-ship, 17 knots. Built by Cia Euskalduna Bilbao as PRINCESA LEOPOLDINA for Cia Nacional de Navegacao Costeira (Brazil). Transferred to Lloyd Brasiliero (Brazil) 1966. Bought by China Navigation Co 1970; renamed CORAL PRINCESS. Refitted at Hong Kong 1970-1 for cruising service. F.V. Yokohama-Naha, 23 July. 1971.

DOMINION FAR EAST LINE, HONG KONG (1963-   )

In 1962 the newly formed Dominion Navigation Co Ltd of Nassau, Bahamas purchased two transatlantic ships, the NOVA SCOTIA and NEWFOUNDLAND of the Furness Warren Line, renaming them FRANCIS DRAKE and GEORGE ANSON. They were refitted and placed in a service between Australia and Japan with H.C. Sleigh of Melbourne as operators.

Seven years later the Lloyd Brasiliero coastal liner PRINCESA ISABEL was purchased, extensively refitted, and renamed MARCO POLO to enter cruising service from Australia early in 1970. The following year the Line's two older ships were sold for breaking up and the regular passenger sailings were discontinued.

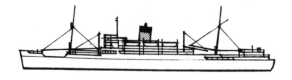

62   FRANCIS DRAKE

'47, (1963-71) 7,743. 441 x 61. Single screw, turbines, 15 knots. 130 passengers. Built by Vickers-Armstrongs, Newcastle as NOVA SCOTIA for Furness Warren Line (Great Britain). M.V. Liverpool-Boston, 2 September 1947. Bought by Dominion Line 1962; renamed FRANCIS DRAKE and re-fitted at Glasgow. F.V. Australia-Japan, March 1963. Route: Melbourne, Sydney, Brisbane, Cairns-Manila, Hong Kong, Keelung, Kobe and Yokohama. Return via Guam and Rabaul. Broken up Kaohsiung, Taiwan 1971.

63   GEORGE ANSON

'48, (1963-71) 7,743. Details as (62). Built by Vickers-Armstrongs as NEWFOUNDLAND for Furness Warren Line. M.V. Liverpool-Boston, 14 February 1948. Bought by Dominion Line 1962; renamed GEORGE ANSON. F.V. Australia-Japan, April 1963. Broken up Kaohsiung 1971.

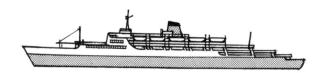

64   MARCO POLO

'62, (1970-   ) 9,232. 478 x 61. Twin screw, motorship, 17 knots. Built by Soc Española de Construccion Naval, Bilbao as PRINCESA ISABEL for Cia Nacional de Navegacao Costeira (Brazil). Transferred to Lloyd Brasiliero (Brazil) 1966. Bought by Dominion Far East Line 1969; renamed MARCO POLO. Towed to Glasgow for refitting 1969-70. Route: Cruising from Melbourne. F.V. 26 June 1970.

MINISTRY OF TRANSPORT, LONDON (1948-60)

With the return of peace in 1945, many vessels were released from wartime shipping controls and refitted to return to their former services. At the same time there was a great increase in the number of British emigrants to the Dominions; many travelling under assisted passage schemes. To provide the necessary berths, vessels of suitable size were acquired by the British Ministry of Transport. Some were owned and registered in the name of the Ministry, while others were chartered as required and refitted to the Ministry's specifications.

The sailings to Australia were made via Suez, but those to New Zealand were routed through the Panama Canal and across the Pacific. The ATLANTIS, the first of the post-war emigrant ships to New Zealand, had been purchased in 1941 and was refitted for the service. The EMPIRE BRENT from the Canadian and Australian services was also refitted and renamed CAPTAIN COOK in 1951 for her voyages to New Zealand. A third ship, the AMARAPOORA of the Australian service, was similarly refitted and renamed CAPTAIN HOBSON the following year.

The level of assisted passage emigration from Britain declined in the nineteen-fifties, and as the need decreased the vessels involved were laid up until, with the withdrawal of the CAPTAIN COOK in 1960, the Government sponsored service in the Pacific was ended.

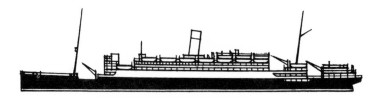

65   ATLANTIS

'13, (1948-52) 15,135. 590 x 57. Triple screw, triple-expansion engines and L.P. turbine, 16 knots. Laid down by Harland & Wolff, Belfast as ANDES for Pacific Steam Navigation Co (Great Britain); transferred to Royal Mail Lines (Great Britain) during construction. Route: Southampton-Buenos Aires. Commissioned as armed merchant cruiser March 1915; participated in sinking of German raider GREIF off Shetland Islands, 28 February 1916. Resumed passenger service 1919. Refitted 1929; renamed ATLANTIS and engaged in world-wide cruising service. Converted to hospital ship 1939; acquired by Ministry of War Transport for carrying exchanged prisoners and war brides. Chartered as emigrant ship to New Zealand under Royal Mail management; F.V. London- New Zealand, 30 November 1948. Broken up on the Clyde 1952.

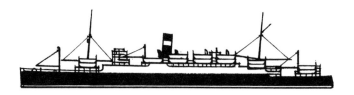

66   CAPTAIN COOK

'25, (1952-60) 13,876. 538 x 66. Twin screw, turbines, 15 knots. Built by Fairfield Shipbuilding & Engineering Co, Govan, Glasgow as LETITIA for Donaldson Line (Great Britain). M.V. Glasgow-Montreal, 24 April 1925. Commissioned as armed merchant cruiser 1939; later served as troopship. Taken over by Canadian Government and converted to hospital ship 1944. Sold to Ministry of Transport 1946; renamed EMPIRE BRENT. Served as troopship to Far East and on Australian emigration service 1948-50. Chartered to New Zealand Government 1951 and refitted as emigrant ship under Donaldson management; renamed CAPTAIN COOK. F.V. Glasgow-New Zealand, 5 February 1952. Diverted to make a number of transatlantic voyages under Donaldson Line charter, summer of 1955. Withdrawn from service February 1960; broken up Inverkeithing.

67 CAPTAIN HOBSON

'20, (1952-8) 9,306. 482 x 59. Single screw, triple-expansion engines, 12.5 knots. Built by Wm Denny & Bros, Dumbarton as AMARAPOORA for Henderson Line (Great Britain). Route: Glasgow, Liverpool-Rangoon. Converted to hospital ship 1939; stationed for three years at Scapa Flow. Bought by Ministry of Transport 1946; chartered to International Refugee Organization for carrying displaced persons. Transferred to New Zealand Government under management of P. Henderson & Co 1951; renamed CAPTAIN HOBSON and refitted on the Clyde. F.V. Glasgow-Wellington, 15 July 1952. Transferred to troopship service at intervals. Laid up at Bombay after twelve New Zealand voyages 1958; broken up Osaka 1959.

2 NEW ZEALAND

UNION STEAMSHIP CO OF NEW ZEALAND, WELLINGTON (1885-1960)

The Union Steam Ship Co of New Zealand Ltd was founded in Dunedin in 1886 to provide shipping services between New Zealand and Australia. An additional service from Wellington to Tahiti was begun in 1909 and was extended to San Francisco the following year. This service became known as the 'Union Line' as distinguished from the Canadian-Australian Royal Mail Line serving Vancouver, a service begun by James Huddart of Melbourne in 1883 and operated solely by the Union S S Co after 1910.

The TAHITI, bought in 1911 for the purpose, was the mainstay of the early Union Line service, but in later years the Company's ships were freely interchanged between the intercolonial service and the two transpacific lines. Two new ships, the MAKURA and NIAGARA, maintained the Vancouver service throughout the First World War, and in 1917 the Company became a member of the P & O Group. The Line's most notable ship, the AORANGI, replaced the MAKURA in 1925, but six years later as a result of Matson Lines competition, the Company combined with the Canadian Pacific Railway to form the Canadian-Australian Line, and the AORANGI and NIAGARA were transferred to the new joint ownership.

After the sinking of the TAHITI in 1930, the P & O liner RAZMAK was acquired, renamed MONOWAI, and entered the San Francisco service for the next two years. Due to financial losses however, the route was discontinued in 1936 and the two ships on the service, the MAKURA and MAUNGANUI, were sold. In the same year the beautiful new AWATEA entered the Tasman Sea service.

The NIAGARA was sunk in 1940 and the C-A Line's service was interrupted the next year when both the AWATEA her replacement, and the AORANGI were requisitioned as transports. The AWATEA was a war loss the following year. Sailings to Vancouver were resumed with the return of the AORANGI in 1948, but in 1953 the seventy-year-old service was finally abandoned.

After the transpacific sailings ended, the MONOWAI continued as the sole survivor in the intercolonial run until her sale in 1960. Since that time the Company's services have been confined to the operation of cargo liners to the Pacific Islands and car ferries between Wellington and Lyttelton. Late in 1971 the ownership of the Company was transferred to Tasman Union Ltd of New Zealand.

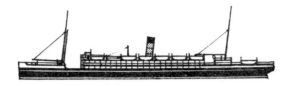

68 MARAMA
'07, (1907-37) 6,437. 436 x 53. Twin screw, triple expansion engines, 15 knots. Built by Caird & Co, Greenock for inter-colonial trade. F.V. Port Chalmers-Lyttelton, Wellington and Sydney, 20 November 1907. Transferred to Sydney-Vancouver service March 1908. Converted to hospital ship at Port Chalmers; F.V. December 1915. Refitted at Vancouver and converted to oil-burning; resumed passenger service Sydney-San Francisco June 1920. Returned to intercolonial service 1922 with occasional voyages as relief vessel on San Francisco service until 1930. Broken up Shanghai 1937.

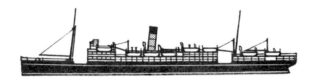

69 MAKURA
'08, (1908-36) 8,075. 466 x 58. Twin screw, triple expansion engines, 16.5 knots. Built by Alexander Stephen & Sons, Linthouse, Glasgow for transpacific service. F.V. Sydney-Auckland, Suva, Honolulu and Vancouver, November 1908. Extensively refitted and converted to oil-burning at San Francisco 1920. Transferred to Sydney, Wellington-San Francisco service March 1925. Broken up Shanghai 1936.

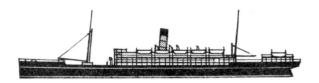

70 TAHITI
'04, (1911-30) 7,585. 460 (R) x 55. Twin screw, triple expansion engines, 17 knots. Built by Alexander Stephen & Sons as PORT KINGSTON for Imperial Direct West India Mail Co (Great Britain). Bought by Union Steam Ship Co 1911; renamed TAHITI. F.V. Sydney, Wellington-Raratonga, Tahiti and San Francisco, December 1911. Served as troopship 1914-19. Refitted and converted to oil-burning; returned to passenger service as relief for MAKURA on Sydney-Vancouver service 1920. Transferred to Union Line service March 1921. Ran down ferry GREYCLIFFE in Wellington harbour with loss of 20 lives, 4 November 1928. Sank in 3,000 fathoms 460 miles south of Raratonga, 17 August 1930 after starboard propeller shaft snapped inboard of stern tube and holed her hull. All passengers and crew saved; taken aboard steamer VENTURA (89).

D

71 MAUNGANUI

'11, (1912-46) 7,527. 447 x 56. Twin screw, quadruple expansion engines, 17 knots. Built by Fairfield Shipbuilding & Engineering Co, Govan, Glasgow for intercolonial service. F.V. Wellington-Lyttelton, Dunedin, Bluff, Hobart and Melbourne, 15 February 1912. Requisitioned as troopship 1914; refitted and converted to oil-burning 1919-21. Transferred to Sydney-San Francisco service until route discontinued in 1936. Converted to hospital ship January 1941; released from service and laid up at Wellington August 1946. Sold to Hellenic Mediterranean Lines for Genoa-Australia emigrant service 1947; renamed CYRENIA and registered in Panama. Broken up Savona 1957.

72 NIAGARA

'13, (1913-40) 13,415. 525 (R) x 66. Triple screw, combination triple expansion engines and L.P. turbine, 17 knots. Built by John Brown & Co, Clydebank, Glasgow. F.V. Sydney-Auckland, Vancouver, 5 May 1913. Passenger service continued throughout World War I. Transferred to Canadian-Australasian Line 1931. Sunk by mine laid by German raider ORION in the approaches to Hauraki Gulf, 19 June 1940.

73 AORANGI

'24, (1925-53) 17,491. 600 x 72. Quadruple screw, motorship, 17 knots, Built by Fairfield Shipbuilding & Engineering Co, Glasgow; the largest British motorship to date. F.V. Vancouver-Auckland, Sydney, 6 February 1925. Transferred to Canadian-Australasian Line 1931. Converted to troopship September 1940; later served as accommodation ship for small craft personnel. Refitted at Sydney; returned to Sydney-Vancouver passenger service August 1948. Laid up at Sydney May 1953; broken up Dalmuir.

74 MONOWAI

'25, (1930-60) 11,037. 519 x 63. Twin screw, quadruple expansion engines and L.P. turbine, 19 knots. Built by Harland & Wolff, Greenock as RAZMAK for P & O Lines Aden-Bombay shuttle service. M.V. London-Aden, 13 March 1925. Bought by Union Steamship Co as replacement for TAHITI 1930; renamed MONOWAI and refitted at Sydney. F.V. Sydney, Wellington-Raratonga, Tahiti and San Francisco, 27 November 1930. Transferred to intercolonial service November 1932. Laid up at Auckland 1936-9. Commissioned as armed merchant cruiser in Royal New Zealand Navy August 1940. Converted to landing ship, infantry, June 1943; later served as troopship. Refitted at Sydney 1946-8; resumed Tasman Sea service January 1949. Broken up Hong Kong 1960.

75 AWATEA

'36, (1936-42) 13,482. 545 x 74. Twin screw, turbines, 22 knots. Built by Vickers-Armstrongs, Barrow-in-Furness for intercolonial service. F.V. Wellington-Auckland, Sydney, 15 September 1936. Broke speed record for Auckland-Sydney run at average of 22.89 knots October 1937. Made a number of voyages in Canadian-Australasian service after sinking of NIAGARA 1940. Requisitioned as troopship September 1941. Collided with escorting destroyer USS BUCK in fog while in convoy out of Halifax, 22 August 1942; exploding depth charges took 7 lives. Destroyer USS INGRAHAM steaming to rescue struck by tanker CHEMUNG and sank with only 10 survivors. Bombed and sunk off Bougie, Algeria, 11 November 1942.

3 AUSTRALIA

HUDDART, PARKER, MELBOURNE (1882-1961)

In 1876 James Huddart and T.J. Parker with two partners formed the firm of Huddart, Parker Ltd trading at Geelong as coal importers and merchants. The head office was moved to Melbourne two years later.

In 1882 three cargo ships were refitted to open a Melbourne-Sydney passenger service, and in September 1889, one of them the BURRUMBEET, took the first sailing on a service to Launceston, Tasmania. In 1893 the company's newest and finest steamer, the TASMANIA, opened a Tasman Sea service to compete with the Union Steam Ship Co of New Zealand.

Four years later the first WESTRALIA was delivered, and with the expanding trade after the turn of the century, three new ships were built, the largest of which was the ZEALANDIA of 1910. This pre-war period marked the high point of the company's passenger trade.

A second WESTRALIA was delivered in 1929, followed three years later by the Line's largest ship, the WANGANELLA, which entered service at a time of depression and declining trade. World War I completely disrupted the company's services and resulted in the loss of the ZEALANDIA to enemy action. The steady decline in passenger traffic continued after the war and the WESTRALIA was sold in 1959 to leave the WANGANELLA as the only ship on the trans-Tasman route. The service ended with her sale three years later.

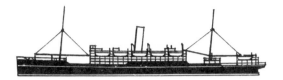

76 ZEALANDIA
'10, (1910-42) 6,683. 410 (R) x 53. Twin screw, quadruple expansion engines, 16 knots. Built by John Brown & Co, Clydebank, Glasgow. Chartered by Union Steam Ship Co of New Zealand for Canadian service on arrival in Australia. F.V. Sydney-Suva, Honolulu and Vancouver, August 1910. Returned to Huddart Parker interstate service April 1913. Requisitioned as troopship May 1918; resumed passenger service December 1919. Transferred to Sydney-Hobart service 1933. Converted to troopship once more, June 1940. Sunk by Japanese dive bombers at Darwin, 19 February 1942.

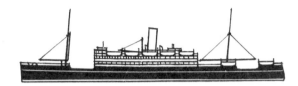

77 WESTRALIA
'29, (1929-59) 8,108. 448 x 60. Twin screw, motorship, 16 knots. Built by Harland & Wolff, Belfast. F.V. Sydney, Melbourne, Adelaide-Fremantle, 28 September 1929. Commissioned as armed merchant cruiser in Royal Australian Navy, January 1940; converted to landing ship, infantry, February 1943. Requisitioned as troopship for post-war service until 1950. Withdrawn from service March 1959. Sold to Asian & Pacific Shipping Co, Suva and converted to sheep carrier at Sydney; renamed DELFINO. Registered in Liberia. Renamed WOOLLAMBI 1960.

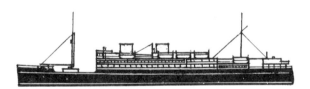

78 WANGANELLA
'31, (1933-61) 9,876. 474 x 64. Twin screw, motorship, 15 knots. Launched by Harland & Wolff December 1929 as ACHIMOTA for Elder Dempster & Co (Great Britain). Laid up at Belfast 1931. Bought by Huddart Parker when Elder Dempster financially unable to accept delivery; renamed WANGANELLA. M.V. Belfast-Australia, November 1932. F.V. Sydney-Milford Sound, Wellington, 12 January 1933. Requisitioned for conversion to hospital ship 1941. Resumed passenger service with a voyage to Vancouver before reopening intercolonial service only to run aground on Barrett's Reef at entrance to Wellington harbour on first trip, 19 January 1947. Hauled off 18 days later; laid up undergoing repair until November 1948. Taken over by McIlwraith, McEacharn, September 1961; continued in Tasman Sea service. Sold to Hang Fung Shipping Co, Hong Kong for charter work and cruising, April 1962. Sold for use as workers' hostel at Manapouri hydro-electric project, Doubtful Sound, New Zealand August 1963. Broken up Kaohsiung 1970.

McILWRAITH, McEACHARN, MELBOURNE (1892-1961)

The firm of McIlwraith, McEacharn Ltd was founded in London in 1875 by Andrew McIlwraith and Malcolm McEacharn. The next year their first ship, the barque SCOTTISH BARD was completed, one of a fleet of sailing ships popularly known as the Scottish Line, which carried emigrants to Queensland under Government contract. In 1879 the chartered steamer STRATHLEVEN was fitted with a refrigeration plant and made the first successful shipment of frozen meat and butter from Australia.

The Company established its first Australian branch office at Melbourne in 1887, followed by offices in the other principal cities of the Colony. In the next few years Australian coastal services were established, later extending to India and Singapore.

A sizeable fleet was built up, and the first large passenger steamer, the KAROOLA, was built in 1909 to be joined four years later by the KATOOMBA. Both were requisitioned for Government service in World War I. In 1935 the Line's largest vessel, the KANIMBLA, was delivered allowing the KAROOLA to be disposed of.

Again in World War II the Line's ships were taken for war services. Although coastal passenger service was resumed after the war, the trade continued to decline and the KANIMBLA was sold in 1961. For a few months the Tasman service was operated with the Huddart Parker liner WANGANELLA, only to end with her sale early in 1962. In 1964 the Company merged its operations with the Adelaide Steamship Co to form Associated Steamships Pty.

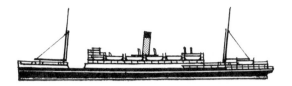

79   KAROOLA
'09, (1909-36) 7,391. 437 x 56. Twin screw, quadruple expansion engines, 16 knots. Built by Harland & Wolff, Belfast. F.V. Sydney-Melbourne, Adelaide, Albany and Fremantle, 25 September 1909. Requisitioned as troopship May 1915; converted to hospital ship three months later. Rescued survivors from HIGHLAND WARRIOR aground on Spanish coast near Cape Ortegal, November 1915. Returned to passenger service June 1919. Laid up at Sydney, May 1936; broken up Shanghai 1937.

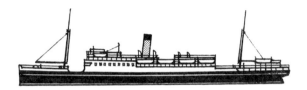

80   KATOOMBA
'13, (1913-46) 9,424. 466 x 60. Triple screw, combination triple expansion engines and L.P. turbine, 16 knots. Built by Harland & Wolff. F.V. Sydney-Melbourne, Adelaide, Albany and Fremantle, 2 September 1913. Requisitioned as troopship, May 1918. Refitted at Sydney 1919-20 and returned to passenger service March 1920. Operated in both Queensland and Western Australia coastal services and in cruising 1932-9. Converted to troopship once more February 1942. Returned to owners 1946; sold to Goulandris Bros of Greece, July 1946 and registered in Panama. Operated by Greek Line; renamed COLUMBIA 1949. Transferred to Bremerhaven-Montreal service June 1950. Laid up at Piraeus March 1958; broken up Nagasaki 1959.

81   KANIMBLA
'36, (1936-61) 11,004. 494 x 66. Twin screw, motorship, 17 knots. Built by Harland & Wolff. M.V. Sydney-Melbourne, Adelaide, 10 June 1936. Commissioned as armed merchant cruiser October 1939. Converted to landing ship, infantry, in Royal Australian Navy May 1943. Retained as transport after war; returned to passenger service December 1950. Stranded in Moreton Bay, 14 June 1952; towed to Brisbane for repairs. On part-time cruising service to Hong Kong and Japan 1958-60. Sold to Pacific Transport Co (Panama) 1961; renamed ORIENTAL QUEEN (250).

AUSTRALIAN STEAMSHIPS PTY, SYDNEY (1854-1945)

The Australian Steamships Proprietary Ltd (Howard Smith Ltd) had its origin in 1854 when Howard Smith started a steamer service between Melbourne and Sydney. This was later extended to the Queensland coast, and by the turn of the century the Australian Steamship Co was operating a sizeable fleet of cargo and small passenger vessels. The Company's largest ship, the CANBERRA, was delivered in 1913 and continued in service until the late 1930s despite the gradual slow-down in trade. After World War II she was laid up and finally sold in 1948 to end the service.

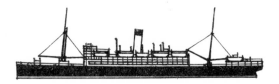

82 CANBERRA

'13, (1913-45) 7,707. 426 x 57. Twin screw, quadruple expansion engines, 15 knots. Built by Alexander Stephen & Sons, Linthouse, Glasgow. Route: Melbourne, Sydney, Brisbane and Queensland ports. Served as troopship 1917-19. Severely damaged by fire at dock in Sydney, 29 May 1925. Laid up at Sydney 1945. Sold to Goulandris Bros of Greece 1948; registered in Panama and refitted for Greek Line transatlantic service. F.V. Piraeus, Genoa-New York 1949. Transferred to Bremerhaven-Montreal service the following year. Sold to Dominican Government 1954; renamed ESPANA. Broken up Dominican Republic 1969.

BURNS, PHILP & CO SYDNEY (1873-1968)

The firm of Burns, Philp & Co Ltd dates back to 1873 when James Burns established
a line of small sailing vessels on the Queensland coast for interstate trade. After
forming a partnership with Robert Philp in 1878, the Company's ships were gradually
changed over to steam and were operated in connection with the Queensland Steam
Shipping Co of 1881 which five years later became part of the Australasian Steam
Navigation Co.

Burns, Philp ships sailed on routes to the South Pacific Islands, Singapore and
China, and the flagship of the fleet in the 1920s was the MARELLA, an ex-German
vessel acquired after World War I. In 1938 the motorship BULOLO was
delivered, only to be taken over for naval duty within a year. After the war she
returned to passenger service, sailing to New Guinea ports until broken up in 1968.
Currently the Company operates a fleet of small motorships trading to the South Sea
Islands.

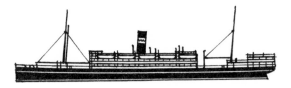

83 MARELLA

'14, (1921-48) 7,475. 452 x 56. Twin screw, quadruple expansion engines, 14 knots. Built by Rieherstieg Schiffswerk, Hamburg as HILDA WOERMANN for Woermann Line (Germany); renamed WAHEHE on completion. Requisitioned by British Government as war reparation 1919; operated by Shaw Savill Line. Bought by Burns, Philp & Co 1921; renamed MARELLA. Route: Australia-Singapore, Hong Kong. Sold to Cia de Nav Baru SA (Panama) 1948; renamed CAPTAIN MARCOS. Renamed LIGURIA 1950; renamed CORSICA 1951. Broken up Belgium 1954.

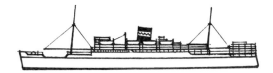

84 BULOLO

'38, (1938-68) 6,397. 412 x 58. Twin screw, motorship, 15 knots. Built by Barclay, Curle & Co; Glasgow. F.V. Sydney, Brisbane-New Guinea ports, 19 November 1938. Commissioned as armed merchant cruiser 1939; converted to landing ship headquarters 1942. D-Day invasion fleet reviewed from her bridge by King George VI. Returned to passenger service 1946. Broken up Kaohsiung 1968.

MELBOURNE STEAMSHIP CO, MELBOURNE (1892-1960)

The Melbourne Coal, Shipping and Engineering Co was formed by a merger of separate business interests in 1884, operating tugs, lighters and excursion steamers in Port Phillips Bay. An interstate shipping service was begun eight years later with the sailing of the 1500 ton steamer BRISBANE.

In 1895 the Company was registered as the Melbourne Shipping Co Ltd and services were expanded to the principal Australian ports. The DUNTROON, the last, and by far the largest vessel built for the Company, was delivered in 1935, replacing the 23-year-old DIMBOOLA. In common with other Australian shipping firms, the decline in coastal traffic after World War II necessitated the sale of the DUNTROON in 1960 to end the Company's shipping interests.

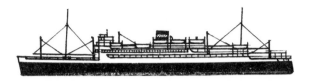

85 DUNTROON

'35, (1935-60) 10,410. 472 x 65. Twin screw, motorship, 18 knots. Built by Swan, Hunter &
Wigham Richardson, Newcastle. F.V. Sydney-Melbourne, Adelaide and Fremantle, 12 October
1935. Converted to troopship February 1942; returned to passenger service 25 August 1950.
Sold to Hong Kong shipbreakers September 1960. Resold to Kie Hock Shipping Co, Hong Kong
1961; renamed TONG HOO. Transferred to Palembang Shipping Co (Panama) 1965. Route:
Burma-Indonesia. Bought by Africa Shipping Co (Panama) 1965; renamed LYDIA 1966 and
placed on pilgrim trade to Jeddah. Laid up at Singapore July 1967; broken up Kaohsiung 1968.

ADELAIDE STEAMSHIP CO, ADELAIDE (1875-1961)

The Adelaide Steamship Co was established in Adelaide, South Australia in 1875. In the following years extensive passenger services were established to West Coast and Queensland ports with a large number of small coastal vessels.

The Company's first large motor liner, the MANUNDA, was built in 1929, followed by the MANOORA six years later. Both ships were requisitioned for service in World War II and at its end returned to a declining trade. The MANUNDA was sold in 1956, and the Company's interstate passenger services came to an end with the sale of the MANOORA five years later.

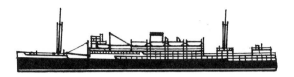

86 MANUNDA

'29, (1929-56) 8,853. 448 x 60. Twin screw, motorship, 17.5 knots. Built by Wm Beardmore & Co, Dalmuir. F.V. Sydney-Melbourne, Adelaide and Fremantle, 28 May 1929. Served as troopship in World War II; returned to passenger service 5 April 1948. Sold to Okada Gumi K.K. (Japan) September 1956; renamed HAKONE MARU. Broken up Japan 1957.

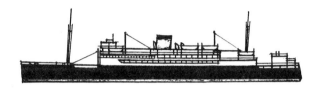

87 MANOORA

'35, (1935-61) 10,952. 482 x 66. Twin screw, motorship, 18 knots. Built by Alexander Stephen & Sons, Linthouse, Glasgow. F.V. Sydney, Melbourne, Adelaide and Fremantle, 11 April 1935. Commissioned as armed merchant cruiser in Royal Australian Navy 1940; forced scuttling of Italian motorship ROMOLO to avoid capture, 6 November 1940. Converted to assault transport; returned to passenger service 5 September 1949. Sold to Republic of Indonesia August 1961; renamed AMBULOMBO. Transferred to PT Affan Raya Line (Indonesia) 1965; renamed AFFAN OCEANA. Returned to Government control 1966; renamed AMBULOMBO. Route: Pilgrim trade to Jeddah.

4   UNITED STATES

MATSON LINES SAN FRANCISCO (1908-71)

The Matson Line was organised in 1901 by Captain William Matson to provide a shipping service between California and Honolulu. The Company's first passenger sailing was made by the steamer LURLINE which left San Francisco 6 June 1908. In the next few years a series of distinctive cargo-passenger, engines-aft steamers was built for the trade.

In 1926 the three ships of the Oceanic Steamship Co, the SIERRA, SONOMA and VENTURA, which had been sailing to Sydney from San Francisco intermittently since 1900, were taken over by the Company and adopted the Matson funnel markings and livery to continue the service as the Matson-Oceanic Line. The following year the new liner MALOLO entered the Honolulu service and soon afterward three even larger ships were ordered. The MARIPOSA, MONTEREY and LURLINE were delivered in 1932-3 to introduce a new standard of luxury to the Pacific. The first two entered the Australian trade as replacements for the Oceanic ships, while the LURLINE joined the MALOLO in the Hawaiian service. Five years later the MALOLO was refitted and renamed MATSONIA.

All four ships served as troopships in World War II. After the war only the MATSONIA returned to service, but she was sold in 1948 and replaced by reactivating the LURLINE. The MARIPOSA and MONTEREY after a long period of idleness were sold, the latter as a troopship. However in 1956 she was repurchased, renamed MATSONIA, and joined the LURLINE on the Hawaii service. At the same time the South Pacific service was reopened with two fast cargo liners rebuilt as passenger ships and renamed MARIPOSA and MONTEREY.

In 1963 the LURLINE was sold to the Chandris Lines and the MATSONIA was renamed a second time as LURLINE to carry on the Hawaiian trade alone. Finally in 1970 she too, was sold, and the Matson Lines' passenger service ended the following year with the sale of the MARIPOSA and MONTEREY to the Pacific Far East Line.

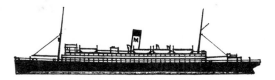

88 SIERRA

'00, (1900-19) (1924-32) 6,135. 417 x 50. Twin screw, triple expansion engines, 16.5 knots. Built by Wm Cramp & Sons, Philadelphia for Oceanic Steamship Co (United States). F.V. San Francisco-Honolulu, Auckland and Sydney, September 1900. Laid up at San Francisco 1907; returned to service on Honolulu route 1910. Extensively refitted; forward funnel removed 1915. Transferred to Sydney service 1915-17. Served as troopship 1917-19. Sold to Polish American Navigation Corp (United States) 1921; renamed GDANSK. Route: New York-Danzig. Repurchased by Oceanic SS Co 1923; renamed SIERRA. Taken over by Matson Lines 1926. Laid up at San Francisco 1932; broken up Japan 1934.

89 VENTURA

'00, (1901-32) 6,253. Details as (88). Built by Wm Cramp & Sons. Route: San Francisco-Australia. Laid up at San Francisco April 1907. Refitted, forward funnel removed and converted to oil-burning 1912; reopened Australia service. Taken over by Matson Lines 1926. Laid up at San Francisco 1932; broken up Japan 1934.

90 SONOMA

'00, (1901-32) 6,279. Details as (88). Built by Wm Cramp & Sons. Route: San Francisco-Australia. Laid up at San Francisco 1907. Refitted 1912; returned to Australia service. Served as troopship 1917-19. Taken over by Matson Lines 1926. Laid up at San Francisco 1932; broken up Japan 1934.

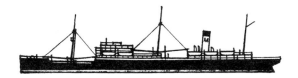

91 WILHELMINA

'09, (1910-32) 6,975. 451 x 54. Single screw, triple expansion engines, 14 knots. Built by Newport News Shipbuilding & Drydock Co, Newport News, Va F.V. San Francisco-Honolulu, 10 February 1910. Served as troopship 1917-19. Transferred to Portland, Seattle-Honolulu service 1928-30. Ceased carrying passengers 1932. Torpedoed and sunk off the coast of England, 2 December 1940.

E

92 MATSONIA

'13, (1914-37) 9,402. 501 x 58. Single screw, triple expansion engines, 15 knots. Built by Newport News SB & DD Co F.V. San Francisco-Honolulu, 28 January 1914. Served as troopship, November 1917 to September 1919. Sold to Alaska Packers Association (United States) March 1937; renamed ETOLIN. Broken up Baltimore 1957.

93 MAUI

'17, (1917-38) 9,801. 501 x 58. Twin screw, turbines, 16 knots. Built by Union Iron Works, San Francisco. M.V. San Francisco-Honolulu, 7 April 1917. Served as troopship 1917-19. Chartered to Panama Pacific Line (United States) for intercoastal cargo service 1938. Converted to troopship once more in Second World War. Broken up 1946.

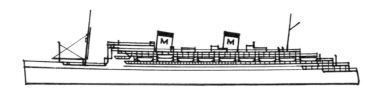

94 MALOLO

'27, (1927-37) 16,435. 582 x 83. Twin screw, turbines, 22 knots. Built by Wm Cramp & Sons, Philadelphia. Struck by Norwegian freighter JACOB CHRISTENSEN while on trials in fog off Rockland, Maine 25 May 1927; towed to New York for extensive repairs. F.V. San Francisco-Honolulu, 16 November 1927. Lanai staterooms added, boats raised two decks 1937; renamed MATSONIA (97).

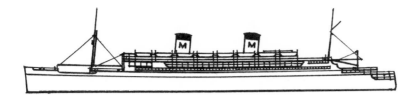

95 MARIPOSA

'32, (1932-53) 18,563. 632 x 79. Twin screw, turbines, 20 knots. Built by Bethlehem Shipbuilding Corp, Quincy, Mass for Matson-Oceanic service. F.V. San Francisco, Los Angeles-Papeete, Auckland, Wellington and Sydney, 2 February 1932. Served as troopship 1941-46. Reconversion halted due to excessive cost; laid up at Alameda 1947. Sold to Home Lines (Panama) 1953; renamed HOMERIC. F.V. Venice-New York, 24 January 1955. Transferred to Caribbean cruising service from New York October 1963.

96 MONTEREY

'32, (1932-52) 18,655. Details as (95). Built by Bethlehem SB Corp, Quincy. F.V. San Francisco-New Zealand, Australia, 3 June 1932. Served as troopship 1941-6. Laid up at Alameda 1946; sold to United States Government for use as troopship 1952. Repurchased by Matson Lines 1956; refitted and renamed MATSONIA (99).

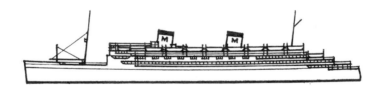

97 MATSONIA

'27, (1938-48) 16,438. Formerly MALOLO (94); renamed MATSONIA December 1937. F.V. San Francisco-Honolulu, 14 January 1938. Served as troopship in Pacific 1941-5; resumed passenger service, 22 May 1946. Laid up at San Francisco April 1948. Sold to Home Lines later in year; renamed ATLANTIC and refitted at Genoa. F.V. Genoa-New York, 14 May 1949. Transferred to National Hellenic American Line (Greece) 1954; renamed QUEEN FREDERICA. Registered as VASILESSA FREIDERIKI. Sold to Chandris Lines November 1965; placed on Southampton-Australia service. Chartered to Sovereign Cruises, London 1968. Laid up at Dartmouth September 1971. Scheduled to be reactivated by Chandris Lines for Mediterranean cruising services from Cannes April 1973

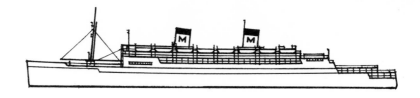

98   LURLINE
'32, (1933-63) 18,564. Details as (95). Built by Bethlehem SB Corp, Quincy as sister of
MARIPOSA and MONTEREY. F.V. San Francisco, Los Angeles-Pacific cruise, 27 January 1933.
Served as troopship 1941-6. Extensively refitted at Alameda; resumed passenger service as replacement for MATSONIA (97) 15 April 1948. Sold to Chandris Lines 1963; renamed ELLINIS (210).

99   MATSONIA .   LURLINE
'32, (1957-70) 18,655. Formerly MONTEREY (96). Repurchased from Government 1956;
renamed MATSONIA. Refitted at Newport News as running mate for LURLINE at a cost of two
and one half times the original cost of the ship. F.V. Los Angeles-Honolulu, 11 June 1957. Renamed LURLINE December 1963 after sale of sister ship. Sold to Chandris Lines 1970; renamed
BRITANIS (212).

AMERICAN MAIL LINE, SEATTLE (1926-40)

The Pacific Coast Steamship Co under the ownership of Goodall, Nelson & Perkins of Seattle, was formed in 1867 to operate steamers on the West Coast of the United States and Canada. In 1916 the Company merged with H.F. Alexander's Pacific Alaska Navigation Co to form the Pacific Steamship Co under the trade name of the Admiral Line.

In 1920 the United States Shipping Board selected the Admiral Line as managing agents for five ex-troopships of the '535' class to operate a Seattle-Orient service. To identify the transpacific service as opposed to the Line's coastal operations, the new organisation was known as the Admiral-Orient Line.

The first sailing from Seattle was made by the WENATCHEE on 9 April 1921. The following year all five ships were renamed as the PRESIDENTS JEFFERSON, JACKSON, McKINLEY, GRANT and MADISON. The Company was purchased by private interests in 1925 and the following year its name was changed to the American Mail Line. A controlling interest was held by the Dollar Line and ships were occasionally interchanged between the two services.

The PRESIDENT MADISON was sold in 1939 and with the outbreak of war, the remaining four ships were converted to Navy attack transports and were eventually broken up at the end of hostilities. Since that time the Line has operated cargo vessels only.

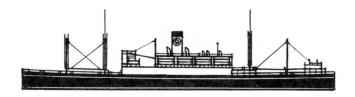

100   PRESIDENT JEFFERSON
'21, (1922-38) 14,124. 535 x 72. Twin screw, turbines, 17 knots. Built by New York Shipbuilding Co, Camden, NJ as '535' Type transport WENATCHEE for United States Shipping Board. Assigned to Admiral-Oriental Line; M.V. Seattle-Orient, 9 April 1921. Renamed PRESIDENT JEFFERSON 1922. Transferred to American Mail Line May 1926. Converted to Army transport 1940; renamed HENRY T ALLEN. Commissioned as Navy transport April 1942. Laid up at Suisun Bay, California, February 1947; broken up 1948.

101   PRESIDENT JACKSON
'21, (1922-38) 14,124. Details as (100). Built by Newport News Shipbuilding & Drydock Co, Newport News, Va as SILVER STATE. Assigned to Admiral-Oriental Line; M.V. Seattle-Orient, 9 July 1921. Renamed PRESIDENT JACKSON 1922. Transferred to American Mail Line 1926. Laid up at Seattle 1938. Commissioned as Navy transport July 1940; renamed USS ZEILIN (AP-9). Laid up in James River July 1946; broken up 1948.

102   PRESIDENT McKINLEY
'21, (1922-38) 14,124. Details as (100). Built by New York SB Co as KEYSTONE STATE. Assigned to Admiral-Orient Line; M.V. Seattle-Orient, 6 August 1921. Renamed PRESIDENT McKINLEY 1922. Transferred to American Mail Line 1926. Converted to Army transport October 1940; renamed J.FRANKLIN BELL. Commissioned as Navy transport April 1942. Laid up at Suisun Bay April 1946; broken up 1948.

103   PRESIDENT GRANT
'21, (1922-36) 14,124. Details as (100). Built by Bethlehem Shipbuilding Corp, Sparrows Point, Md as PINE TREE STATE. Delivered 3 November 1921; assigned to Admiral-Oriental Line. Renamed PRESIDENT GRANT 1922. Transferred to American Mail Line 1926. Laid up at Seattle 1936. Commissioned as Navy transport August 1940; renamed USS HARRIS (AP-8). Laid up in James River July 1946; broken up 1948.

104   PRESIDENT MADISON
'21, (1922-39) 14,124. Details as (100). Built by New York SB Co as BAY STATE. Delivered 18 November 1921; assigned to Admiral-Oriental Line. Renamed PRESIDENT MADISON 1922. Transferred to American Mail Line 1926. Capsized at dock in Seattle, 24 March 1933; raised and refit completed November 1934. Sold to Filipino interests 1939; renamed PRESIDENT QUEZON. Ran aground on coast of Japan while on delivery voyage January 1940 and became a total loss.

DOLLAR LINE, SAN FRANCISCO (1924-38)

The Dollar Steamship Line was established in 1910 by Captain Robert Dollar who had been engaged in logging operations in the Northwest, and starting in 1901, had built up a fleet trading to the Orient. In 1923 the Company bought seven war-surplus '502' Type 'President' liners from the United States Shipping Board and began a westbound round-the-world service. The first sailing was taken by the PRESIDENT HARRISON which left San Francisco 5 January 1924. The following year an additional five 'President' liners of the '535' Type were taken over from the Pacific Mail Steamship Co and were assigned to a transpacific service.

In 1929 the Panama Pacific liners MANCHURIA and MONGOLIA were purchased and entered the round-the-world service as the PRESIDENT JOHNSON and PRESIDENT FILLMORE, and two years later two large and luxurious vessels, the PRESIDENT HOOVER and PRESIDENT COOLIDGE, were built to compete on the transpacific trade with the new NYK and Canadian Pacific liners. Unfortunately, the PRESIDENT HOOVER ran aground in the Far East and became a total loss after only six years of service.

The economic depression of the 1930s resulted in loss of trade and financial troubles for the Company, and in 1938 the United States Government took over its management and reorganised the firm as the American President Lines.

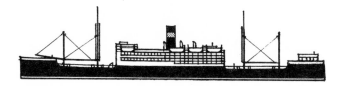

PRESIDENT HARRISON
'20 (1924-41) see (115)

105 PRESIDENT HAYES
'20, (1924-40) 10,533. 523 x 62. Twin screw, triple expansion engines, 14 knots. Built by New York Shipbuilding Co, Camden NJ as '502' Type transport CREOLE STATE for United States Shipping Board. Assigned to United States Mail Steamship Co; M.V. New York-London December 1920. Transferred to Pacific Mail Steamship Co 1921. F.V. San Francisco-Calcutta, 3 February 1921. Bought by Dollar Line September 1923; renamed PRESIDENT HAYES 1924. F.V. San Francisco-westbound round-the-world, 2 February 1924. Transferred to American President Lines 1938; renamed PRESIDENT TYLER (116) 1940.

106 PRESIDENT ADAMS
'21, (1924-40) 10,496. Details as (105). Built by New York SB Co as CENTENNIAL STATE. Assigned to United States Mail; M.V. New York-London June 1921. Transferred to United States Lines August 1921; renamed PRESIDENT ADAMS May 1922. Bought by Dollar Line September 1923. F.V. San Francisco-round-the world, 1 March 1924. Grounded at eastern end of Panama Canal, 11 January 1929; laid up four months for repairs at San Francisco. Transferred to American President Lines 1938; renamed PRESIDENT GRANT (117) 1940.

107 PRESIDENT GARFIELD
'21, (1924-40) 10,496. Details as (105)..Built by New York SB Co as BLUE HEN STATE. Assigned to United States Mail; M.V. New York-London June 1921. Transferred to United States Lines 1921; renamed PRESIDENT GARFIELD 1922. Bought by Dollar Line 1923. F.V. San Francisco-round-the-world, 15 March 1924. Transferred to American President Lines 1938; renamed PRESIDENT MADISON (118) 1940.

108 PRESIDENT POLK
'21, (1924-40) 10,496. Details as (105). Built by New York SB Co as GRANITE STATE. Assigned to Pacific Mail; F.V. San Francisco-Orient, 16 April 1921. Transferred to United States Lines 1922; F.V. New York-Bremen April 1922. Renamed PRESIDENT POLK August 1922. Bought by Dollar Line 1923. F.V. San Francisco-round-the-world, 29 March 1924. Transferred to American President Lines 1938; renamed PRESIDENT TAYLOR (119) 1940.

109 PRESIDENT MONROE
'20, (1924-40) 10,533. Details as (105). Built by New York SB Co as PANHANDLE STATE. Assigned to United States Mail; M.V. New York-London September 1920. Transferred to United States Lines 1921; renamed PRESIDENT MONROE 1922. Bought by Dollar Line 1923. F.V. San Francisco-round-the-world, 14 April 1924. Transferred to American President Lines 1938; renamed PRESIDENT BUCHANAN (120) 1940.

110 PRESIDENT VAN BUREN

'20, (1924-40) 10,533. Details as (105). Built by New York SB Co as OLD NORTH STATE.
Assigned to United States Mail; M.V. New York-London November 1920. Transferred to United
States Lines 1921; renamed PRESIDENT VAN BUREN 1922. Bought by Dollar Line 1923. F.V.
San Francisco-round-the-world, 10 May 1924. Transferred to American President Lines 1938;
renamed PRESIDENT FILLMORE (121) 1940.

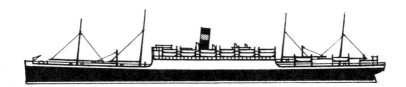

111 PRESIDENT JOHNSON

'04, (1929-41) 15,445. 616 x 65. Twin screw, quadruple expansion engines, 16 knots. Laid down
by New York Shipbuilding Co, Camden, NJ as MINNEKAHDA for Atlantic Transport Line (United
States); completed as MANCHURIA for Pacific Mail Steamship Co Bought by Atlantic Transport
Line as wartime replacement 1916. Transferred to American Line 1919; F.V. New York-Hamburg,
December 1919. Transferred to Panama Pacific Line (United States) for intercoastal service 1923.
Bought by Dollar Line 1929; renamed PRESIDENT JOHNSON. F.V. San Francisco-westbound
round-the-world, 22 February 1929. Transferred to American President Lines 1938. Converted to
troopship November 1941; returned to owners March 1946. Sold to Transmar (Panama) January
1947; renamed SANTA CRUZ. Sold to Tagus Navegacion Cia (Portugal) 1949; renamed TAGUS.
Broken up Savona 1952.

112 PRESIDENT FILLMORE

'04, (1930-40) 15,445. Details as (111). Laid down by New York SB Co as MINNELORA for
Atlantic Transport Line; completed as MONGOLIA for Pacific Mail. Bought by Atlantic Transport
Line 1916; transferred to American Line 1919 and to Panama Pacific Line 1923. Bought by Dollar
Line 1929; renamed PRESIDENT FILLMORE. F.V. San Francisco-round-the-world, 7 February
1930. Transferred to American President Lines 1938. Sold to Cia Trasatlantica Centroamericana
(Panama) February 1940; renamed PANAMANIAN. Laid up at Hong Kong 1946; broken up
Shanghai 1947.

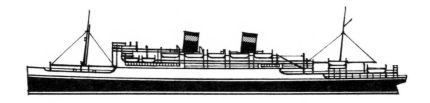

113 PRESIDENT HOOVER

'31, (1931-7) 21,936. 654 x 81. Twin screw, turbo-electric, 21 knots. Built by Newport News Shipbuilding & Drydock Co, Newport News, Va F.V. San Francisco-Honplulu, Manila, 28 August 1931. Grounded near Hoishoto Island off southern tip of Taiwan, 11 December 1937. Broken up where she lay after salvage attempts failed.

114 PRESIDENT COOLIDGE

'31, (1931-42) 21,936. Details as (113). Built by Newport News SB & DD Co F.V. San Francisco-Far East, 6 November 1931. Collided with, and sank tanker FRANK H. BUCK while outbound in Golden Gate, 6 March 1937. Transferred to American President Lines 1938. Converted to troop-ship January 1942. Struck minefield at entrance to harbour of Espiritu Santo, New Hebrides and sank in deep water, 26 October 1942. Only two lives lost of 5,150 troops embarked.

AMERICAN PRESIDENT LINES, SAN FRANCISCO (1938-   )

In 1938 the United States Government took over the management of the financially troubled Dollar Line which was reorganised as the American President Lines. The fleet consisted of seven '502' and five '535' Type standard 'President' liners, all built between 1920-2, plus the elderly PRESIDENT JOHNSON and PRESIDENT FILLMORE and the nearly new PRESIDENT COOLIDGE.

Seven ships were ordered as replacements, and in 1940-1 the PRESIDENTS JACKSON, MONROE, HAYES, GARFIELD, VAN BUREN and POLK were completed and entered the round-the-world service. The seventh, the PRESIDENT ADAMS, was requisitioned as a Navy transport before completion. To avoid duplication, six of the seven '502s' were renamed. The outbreak of war in Europe disrupted the Line's services, and a number of the older ships were sold or converted to transports. After the attack on Pearl Harbor, all the Company's remaining ships were taken over for war duties.

At the end of the war only two ships, the PRESIDENT MONROE and PRESIDENT POLK, returned to the Company's round-the-world service. Two additional ships, the PRESIDENT CLEVELAND and PRESIDENT WILSON, laid down as transports, were completed in 1947-8 for the transpacific service and three more were ordered for delivery in 1951 only to be taken over as transports for the Korean War.

A third ship for the Pacific service, the Panama Railroad Co's PANAMA, was purchased in 1957 and renamed PRESIDENT HOOVER. In addition, the Hawaiian Steamship Co's LEILANI was bought in 1960 and after extensive remodelling, entered service as the PRESIDENT ROOSEVELT.

In 1964 the PRESIDENT HOOVER was sold to the Chandris Line and six years later the PRESIDENT ROOSEVELT went to the same buyers. By 1972 the PRESIDENT CLEVELAND and PRESIDENT WILSON, along with the Pacific Far East Line's MARIPOSA and MONTEREY, were the only passenger liners sailing under the American flag.

115   PRESIDENT HARRISON
'20, (1924-41) 10,496. 523 x 62. Twin screw, triple expansion engines, 14 knots. Built by New York Shipbuilding Co, Camden, NJ as Type '502' transport WOLVERINE STATE for United States Shipping Board; assigned to Pacific Mail Steamship Co. F.V. San Francisco-Calcutta, 25 February 1921. Bought by Dollar Line 1923; renamed PRESIDENT HARRISON. Inaugurated round-the-world service; F.V. from San Francisco, 5 January 1924. Transferred to American President Lines 1938. Converted to troopship; evacuated US Marines from Shanghai November 1941. Captured by Japanese forces after grounding in East China Sea, 8 December 1941; renamed KAKKO MARU, later KACHIDOKI MARU. Torpedoed and sunk by USS PAMPANITO in South China Sea, 12 September 1944.

116   PRESIDENT TYLER
'20, (1940-6) 10,533. Formerly PRESIDENT HAYES (105) Dollar Line. Transferred to American President Lines 1938; renamed PRESIDENT TYLER 1940. Converted to troopship January 1942. Refit as Army hospital ship begun February 1945; renamed HOWARD A. McCURDY. Work stopped at end of war; renamed PRESIDENT TYLER. Laid up in Hudson River April 1947; broken up 1957.

117   PRESIDENT GRANT
'21, (1940-4) 10,496. Formerly PRESIDENT ADAMS (106) Dollar Line. Transferred to President Lines 1938; renamed PRESIDENT GRANT 1940. Converted to troopship March 1942. Stranded and lost on Ulna Reed off the coast of New Guinea, 26 February 1944.

118   PRESIDENT MADISON
'21, (1940-2) 10,496. Formerly PRESIDENT GARFIELD (107) Dollar Line. Transferred to American President Lines 1938; renamed PRESIDENT MADISON 1940. Commissioned as Navy transport April 1942; renamed USS KENMORE (AP-62). Converted to Navy hospital ship February 1944; renamed USS REFUGE (AH-11). Laid up at Olympia, Washington July 1946; broken up 1948.

119   PRESIDENT TAYLOR
'21, (1940-2) 10,496. Formerly PRESIDENT POLK (108) Dollar Line. Transferred to American President Lines 1938; renamed PRESIDENT TAYLOR 1940. Converted to troopship December 1941. Stranded and abandoned off Canton Island, 14 February 1942.

120 PRESIDENT BUCHANAN
'20, (1940-3) 10,533. Formerly PRESIDENT MONROE (109) Dollar Line. Transferred to
American President Lines 1938; renamed PRESIDENT BUCHANAN 1940. Converted to troopship
March 1942. Refitted as Army hospital ship November 1943; renamed EMILY H.M.WEDER.
Resumed service as troopship November 1945; renamed PRESIDENT BUCHANAN. Laid up at
Suisun Bay December 1946; broken up 1947.

121 PRESIDENT FILLMORE
'20, (1940-4) 10,533. Formerly PRESIDENT VAN BUREN (110) Dollar Line. Transferred to
American President Lines 1938; renamed PRESIDENT FILLMORE 1940. Converted to troopship
February 1942. Refitted as Army hospital ship June 1944; renamed MARIGOLD. Laid up at
Suisun Bay June 1946; broken up 1948.

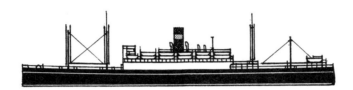

122 PRESIDENT CLEVELAND
'21, (1922-42) 14,124. 535 x 72. Twin screw, turbines, 17 knots. Built by Newport News Ship-
building & Dry Dock Co, Newport News, Va as Type '535' transport GOLDEN STATE for United
States Shipping Board; assigned to Pacific Mail Steamship Co F.V. San Francisco-Honolulu,
Yokohama, Kobe, Shanghai, Hong Kong and Manila, 19 March 1921. Renamed PRESIDENT
CLEVELAND 1922. Bought by Dollar Line April 1925; F.V. San Francisco-Orient, 21 March 1925.
Transferred to American President Lines 1938. Converted to Army transport 1941; renamed
GENERAL TASKER H. BLISS. Commissioned as Navy transport August 1942; renamed USS
TASKER H. BLISS (AP-42). Torpedoed and sunk by German submarine U-130 during assault
landing at Fedala, Morocco, 12 November 1942.

123 PRESIDENT WILSON
'21, (1922-40) 15,124. Details as (122). Built by New York Shipbuilding Co, Camden, NJ as
EMPIRE STATE; assigned to Pacific Mail. F.V. San Francisco-Orient, 30 July 1921. Renamed
PRESIDENT WILSON 1922. Bought by Dollar Line 1925; F.V. San Francisco-Orient, 11 July
1925. Transferred to round-the-world service 1929. Transferred to American President Lines 1938.
Sold to Berge & Co (Spain) 1940; renamed MARIA PIPA. Resold to Ybarra y Cia. (Spain) 1940;
renamed CABO DE HORNOS. Broken up Aviles, Spain 1959.

124 PRESIDENT LINCOLN
'21, (1922-40) 14,124. Details as (122). Built by New York SB Co as HOOSIER STATE; assigned
to Pacific Mail. F.V. San Francisco-Orient, 12 October 1921. Renamed PRESIDENT LINCOLN
1922. Bought by Dollar Line 1925; F.V. San Francisco-Orient, 16 May 1925. Transferred to
American President Lines 1938. Sold to Berge & Co 1940; renamed MARIA DEL CARMEN.
Resold to Ybarra y Cia 1940; renamed CABO DE BUENA ESPERANZA. Broken up Spain 1958.

125 PRESIDENT TAFT

'21, (1922-42) 14,124. Details as (122). Built by Bethlehem Shipbuilding Corp, Sparrows Point, Maryland as BUCKEYE STATE; assigned to Pacific Mail. Renamed PRESIDENT TAFT 1922. F.V. San Francisco-Orient, 12 September 1922. Bought by Dollar Line 1925; F.V. San Francisco-Orient, 27 June 1925. Transferred to American President Lines 1938. Converted to Army transport June 1941; renamed GENERAL WILLARD A. HOLBROOK. Laid up in James River November 1949; broken up 1957.

126 PRESIDENT PIERCE

'21, (1922-42) 14,124. Details as (122). Built by Bethlehem SB Corp, Sparrows Point as HAWKEYE STATE; assigned to Pacific Mail. Renamed PRESIDENT PIERCE 1922. F.V. San Francisco-Orient, 4 October 1922. Bought by Dollar Line 1925; F.V. San Francisco-Orient, 13 June 1925. Transferred to American President Lines 1938. Converted to Army transport July 1941; renamed GENERAL HUGH L. SCOTT. Commissioned as Navy transport August 1942; renamed USS HUGH L. SCOTT (AP-43). Torpedoed and sunk by U-130 off Fedala, 12 November 1942.

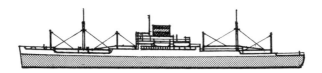

127 PRESIDENT JACKSON

'40, (1940-1) 9.255. 492 x 70. Single screw, turbines, 17 knots. 96 passengers. Built by Newport News Shipbuilding & Drydock Co, Newport News, Va M.V. San Francisco-westbound round-the-world, 23 November 1940; routed via Capetown as wartime measure. Commissioned as Navy transport June 1941; renamed USS PRESIDENT JACKSON (AP-37). Operated by Military Sea Transportation Service after war. Laid up in Navy Reserve Fleet, San Francisco 1955; moved to Suisun Bay 1958.

128 PRESIDENT MONROE

'40, (1941-64) 9,255. Details as (127). Built by Newport News SB & DD Co M.V. San Francisco-round-the-world, 17 January 1941. Converted to troopship January 1942. Commissioned as Navy transport August 1943; renamed USS PRESIDENT MONROE (AP-103). Returned to passenger service November 1946. Sold to John S. Latsis, Athens 1965; renamed MARIANNA V. Registered in Panama.

129 PRESIDENT HAYES

'41, (1941) 9,255. Details as (127). Built by Newport News SB & DD Co M.V. San Francisco-round-the-world, 11 April 1941. Commissioned as Navy transport July 1941; renamed USS PRESIDENT HAYES (AP-39). Laid up in Navy Reserve Fleet 1953; moved to Suisun Bay 1958.

130 PRESIDENT GARFIELD
'41, (1941) 9,260. Details as (127). Built by Newport News SB & DD Co M.V. San Francisco-round-the-world, 25 April 1941. Converted to troopship November 1941. Commissioned as Navy transport May 1942; renamed USS THOMAS JEFFERSON (AP-60). Laid up in Navy Reserve Fleet 1955; moved to Suisun Bay 1958.

131 PRESIDENT VAN BUREN
'41, (1941-2) 9,260. Details as (127). Built by Newport News SB & DD Co M.V. San Francisco-round-the-world, 11 October 1941. Commissioned as Navy transport January 1942; renamed USS THOMAS R STONE (AP-59). Torpedoed 7 November 1942; towed 150 miles to Algiers but drifted on beach in storm. Broken up 1944 after salvage efforts failed.

132 PRESIDENT POLK
'41, (1946-64) 9,260. Details as (127). Built by Newport News SB & DD Co M.V. New York-San Francisco, 6 November 1941. Converted to troopship at San Francisco December 1941. Commissioned as Navy transport September 1943; renamed USS PRESIDENT POLK (AP-104). Returned to passenger service August 1946. Sold to Ganderos del Mar (Liberia) 1965; renamed GAUCHO MARTIN FIERRO. Renamed MINOTAUROS 1966. Broken up Kaohsiung 1970.

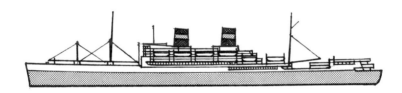

133 PRESIDENT CLEVELAND
'47, (1947-   ) 15,456. 610 x 76. Twin screw, turbo-electric, 19 knots. Laid down as Type P2 transport by Bethlehem Alameda Shipyard, Alameda, Calif; redesigned and completed as first American post-war liner. M.V. San Francisco-Orient, 15 December 1947. Withdrawn from service January 1973.

134 PRESIDENT WILSON
'48, (1948-   ) 15,446. Details as (133). Built by Bethlehem Alameda Shipyard. M.V. San Francisco-Orient, 27 April 1948. Scheduled to be withdrawn from service after final round-the-world cruise, April 1973

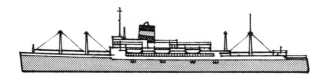

135 PRESIDENT HOOVER

'39, (1957-64) 10,021. 494 x 64. Twin screw, turbines, 17 knots. Built by Bethlehem Steel Co, Quincy, Mass as PANAMA for Panama Railroad Co (United States). Route: Cristobal-New York. Converted to Army transport June 1941; renamed JAMES PARKER. Resumed passenger service June 1946; renamed PANAMA. Bought by American President Lines 1957; renamed PRESIDENT HOOVER. F.V. San Francisco, Los Angeles-Far East, 11 February 1957. Sold to Chandris Lines December 1964; renamed REGINA. Refitted at Piraeus for cruising service 1965. Registry transferred to Panama 1967.

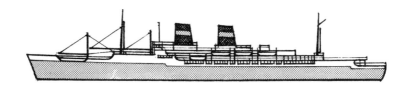

136 PRESIDENT ROOSEVELT

'44, (1962-70) 18,920. Formerly LEILANI (140) Hawaiian Steamship Co Bought by American President Lines 1960; renamed PRESIDENT ROOSEVELT. Extensively remodelled at Seattle 1961-2. F.V. San Francisco, Los Angeles-Orient, 10 May 1962. Sailed on first round-the-world cruise January 1966. Sold to Chandris Lines March 1970; renamed ATLANTIS. Extensively refitted once more at Piraeus 1970-1 for cruising service from New York and Port Everglades to Bahamas. Sold to Eastern Steamship Lines of Miami, January 1972; renamed EMERALD SEAS and registered in Panama. Route: Miami-Nassau.

LOS ANGELES STEAMSHIP CO, LOS ANGELES (1922-32)

The Los Angeles Steamship Co was organised in 1920 to operate the recently purchased coastal steamers YALE and HARVARD. In 1922 the Company chartered two former German liners from the United States Shipping Board and refitted them for a service between Los Angeles and Honolulu. The first sailing was made by the CITY OF LOS ANGELES, built as the Norddeutscher Lloyd liner GROSSER KURFURST. Her running mate, the CITY OF HONOLULU, originally the NDL's FRIEDRICH DER GROSSE, followed the next month only to catch fire on her return voyage 600 miles off the California coast. She was abandoned and sunk by gun-fire as a menace to navigation. As a replacement the 29-year-old US Army transport SHERMAN was purchased, renamed CALAWAII, and placed in service the following year.

In 1924 the Company purchased the PRESIDENT ARTHUR, once the Hamburg American Line's KIAUTSCHOU, and renamed her CITY OF HONOLULU (II). Entering service in 1927, she too was badly damaged by fire three years later at her berth in Honolulu. Though she managed to return to Los Angeles under her own power, she was laid up and later sold for breaking up.

The Company was taken over by Matson Lines late in 1930 but as a result of the economic depression, the CALAWAII and CITY OF LOS ANGELES were also laid up soon afterward and were eventually sold to Japanese breakers.

F

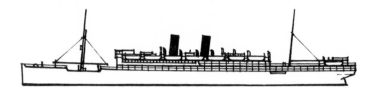

137 CITY OF LOS ANGELES

'99, (1922-33) 13,182. 575 x 62. Twin screw, quadruple expansion engines, 16 knots. Built by F. Schichau, Danzig as GROSSER KURFURST for Norddeutscher Lloyd (Germany). Route: Bremerhaven-New York; transferred to Australian service November 1900. Interned in New York at outbreak of World War I. Converted to transport 1917; renamed AEOLUS. Refitted at Baltimore by United States Shipping Board and chartered to Munson Line (United States) February 1920; F.V. New York-Buenos Aires, 1 December 1920. Rammed and sank British freighter ZERO in South Atlantic March 1922. Transferred to Los Angeles Steamship Co, April 1922; renamed CITY OF LOS ANGELES. F.V. Los Angeles-Honolulu, 11 September 1922. Extensively refitted 1923-4; turbines installed, speed increased to 17 knots. Laid up at San Diego 1933; broken up Japan 1937.

138 CALAWAII

'93, (1923-32) 7,271. 445 (R) x 49. Twin screw, triple expansion engines, 13.5 knots. Built by Harland & Wolff, Belfast as MOBILE for Elder Dempster Line (Great Britain). M.V. London-New York, 20 January 1893. Bought by Atlantic Transport Line (Great Britain) October 1896. Bought by United States Government 1898; renamed SHERMAN and converted to Army transport for Spanish-American War service. After war employed in trooping service to Philippines. Bought by Los Angeles Steamship Co 1922; renamed CALAWAII and refitted for passenger service. F.V. Los Angeles-Honolulu February 1923. Laid up at San Diego 1932; broken up Japan 1933.

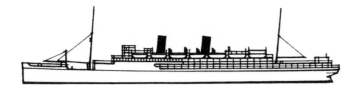

139 CITY OF HONOLULU

'00, (1927-30) 10,680. 540 x 60. Twin screw, quadruple expansion engines, 17 knots. Built by A.G. Vulkan, Stettin as KIAUTSCHOU for Hamburg American Line (Germany). Route: Germany-Far East. Bought by Norddeutscher Lloyd 1903; renamed PRINZESS ALICE. Seized by United States Government and converted to transport 1917; renamed PRINCESS MATOIKA. Chartered to United States Mail Steamship Co F.V. New York-Naples, Genoa, 8 March 1921. Transferred to United States Lines five months later; renamed PRESIDENT ARTHUR 1922. Bought by Los Angeles Steamship Co 1924; renamed CITY OF HONOLULU and extensively refitted. F.V. Los Angeles-Honolulu, 4 June 1927. Badly damaged by fire at dock in Honolulu, 25 May 1930. Returned to Los Angeles under own power and laid up October 1930; broken up Japan 1933.

HAWAIIAN STEAMSHIP CO, SAN FRANCISCO (1957-8)

The Hawaiian Steamship Co was formed in 1956 as a subsidiary of Textron Inc to provide competition for the long-established Matson Lines in the post-war California-Hawaii trade. The American Export Lines' transatlantic liner LA GUARDIA which had been laid up, was purchased, refitted and renamed LEILANI.

The service was opened in February 1957 but was not successful and was terminated in December of the following year. The LEILANI was again laid up and was eventually bought at auction by the American President Lines.

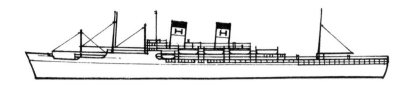

140 LEILANI
'44, (1957-8) 18,298. 622 x 75. Twin screw, turbines, 20 knots. Built by Federal Shipbuilding &
Drydock Co, Kearny, NJ as Navy transport GENERAL W.P. RICHARDSON. (AP-118).
Chartered by American Export Lines (United States) 1948; refitted at Pascagoula, Miss and
renamed LA GUARDIA. F.V. New York-Naples, Genoa, 27 May 1949. Returned to Government
control December 1951; after a period of troopship service to Korea, laid up in James River
November 1952. Bought by Textron Inc and chartered to Hawaiian Steamship Co 1956; refitted
at Camden, NJ and renamed LEILANI. F.V. San Francisco-Honolulu, 5 February 1957. Laid up
at San Francisco December 1958; repossessed by US Maritime Administration May 1959. Sold to
American President Lines 1960; renamed PRESIDENT ROOSEVELT (136).

PACIFIC FAR EAST LINE, SAN FRANCISCO (1971-   )

The Pacific Far East Line, one of the first American shipping companies organised after the Second World War, was founded in July 1946 to operate a transpacific cargo service between California and the Far East. Sailings were begun with five cargo ships under bare boat charter. These were increased in the next twenty years to a fleet of thirteen cargo liners of which nine were of the fast, modern 'Mariner' type. All had the word 'Bear' as a suffix to their names.

By 1971 the Company was operating one of the new LASH lighter-carrying freighters, the THOMAS E. CUFFE, with five more under construction to serve ports in Australia and New Zealand. In the same year the Matson Lines' passenger liners MARIPOSA and MONTEREY were purchased to continue in cruising service and on the California-Australia route under the new ownership.

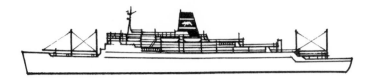

141   MARIPOSA
'53, (1956-   ) 14,812. 563 x 70. Single screw, turbines, 20 knots. Built by Bethlehem Steel Co, Quincy, Mass as cargo liner PINE TREE STATE. Bought by Matson Lines and refitted for passenger service at Portland, Oregon 1956; renamed MARIPOSA. F.V. San Francisco, Los Angeles-Papeete, Auckland, Wellington and Sydney, 27 October 1956. Bought by Pacific Far East Line 1971.

142   MONTEREY
'52, (1957-   ) 14,799. Details as (141). Built by Bethlehem Shipbuilding Corp, Sparrows Point, Maryland as cargo liner FREE STATE MARINER. Bought by Matson Lines and refitted 1956; renamed MONTEREY. F.V. San Francisco, Los Angeles-New Zealand, Australia, 8 January 1957. Bought by Pacific Far East Line 1971.

5 JAPAN

NIPPON YUSEN KAISHA, TOKYO (1885-1960)

The Nippon Yusen Kaisha (Japan Mail Steamship Co) was established in 1885 by the joining of two rival shipping firms, Yubin Kisin Mitsubishi Kaisha and Kiodo Unyu Kaisha. Each company contributed 29 ships to the combined fleet.

Sailings to Hawaii were begun in the same year under Government contract, and by 1894 over 27,000 emigrants had been carried to the Islands. The first transpacific sailing was made from Kobe to Seattle by the MIIKE MARU on 1 August 1896 to provide a maritime outlet for the recently completed Great Northern Railway. Two years later a San Francisco service was added, and routes were also established to Europe, India, Australia and the Asiatic mainland to form a world-wide network.

In February 1926 the Company was combined with Toyo Kisen Kaisha, one of the largest Japanese shipping lines, and took over the operation of the TKK fleet which included five passenger liners on the San Francisco service and four serving the west coast of South America. Three outstanding new liners, the ASAMA MARU, TAT-SUTA MARU and CHICHIBU MARU were built in 1929-30 and were placed in the Kobe-San Francisco service where they broke the speed record for the passage. By 1935 the Company had 85 vessels in service totalling 625,000 gross tons.

After the TERUKUNI MARU was sunk by a magnetic mine in the English Channel in 1939, all sailings to Europe were cancelled and two new ships, the NITTA MARU and YAWATA MARU, built for the European service, were diverted to the transpacific trade. A third sister, the KASUGA MARU, was rebuilt as the escort aircraft carrier TAIYO before completion. In addition, two ships, the MIIKE MARU and AKI MARU, ordered for the Seattle service, were requisitioned by the armed forces, while the 28,000 ton liners KASHIHARA MARU and IZUMO MARU, laid down for the transpacific trade, were taken over in June 1941 and completed as the carriers JUNYO and HIYO.

With the outbreak of hostilities in 1941 the entire fleet was assigned to war service and was systematically destroyed by American submarines and 'planes. By the end of the war the HIKAWA MARU, converted to a hospital ship, was the sole surviving passenger liner. She returned to the Seattle service in 1950, but no new ships were built to join her, and the Line's Pacific passenger services ended with her sale in 1960.

143 KAGA MARU
'01, (1901-30) 6,301. 445 (R) x 49. Twin screw, triple expansion engines, 14 knots. Built by
Mitsubishi Dockyard, Nagasaki; delivered 15 May 1901. Route: Hong Kong, Japan-Seattle.
Served as troopship in Russo-Japanese War 1904-05. Laid up at Kobe 1930; broken up 1934.

144 IYO MARU
'01, (1901-30) 6,320. Details as (143). Built by Mitsubishi Dockyard; delivered 16 November 1901.
Route: Seattle service. Served as troopship 1904-05. Laid up 1930; broken up 1933.

145 AKI MARU
'03, (1903-30) 6,023. Details as (143). Built by Mitsubishi Dockyard; delivered 13 February 1903.
Route: Hong Kong, Japan-Seattle. Served as troopship 1904-05; later transferred to Australia
service. Diverted to wartime service 1917-22. Laid up 1930; broken up 1934.

146 KAMO MARU
'08, (1917-44) 8,524. 474 (R) x 54. Triple screw, triple expansion engines, 15 knots. Built by
Mitsubishi Dockyard; delivered 8 July 1908. Route: Japan-Europe. Transferred to Seattle service
1917-22; to Australia service 1930. Torpedoed and sunk by USS TINOSA off west coast of Japan,
3 July 1944.

147 MISHIMA MARU
'08, (1909-34) 7,905. Details as (146) except twin screw. Built by Kawasaki Dockyard, Kobe;
delivered 25 December 1908. Route: Japan-Australia. Diverted to wartime service 1917-22; transferred to Seattle service 1929. Broken up 1934.

148 ATSUTA MARU . ATUTA MARU
'09, (1917-42) 7,974. Details as (147). Built by Mitsubishi Dockyard; delivered 3 March 1909.
Route: Japan-Europe via Suez Canal. Transferred to Seattle service September 1917-March 1922;
transferred to Australia service 1930. Renamed ATUTA MARU 1938. Torpedoed and sunk by
USS POMPANO off Okinawa, 30 May 1942.

149 KITANO MARU

'09, (1917-42) 8,512. Details as (147). Built by Mitsubishi Dockyard; delivered 26 April 1909. Route: Japan-Europe. Transferred to Australia service 1917-22 and again in 1930. Became a war casualty 27 March 1942.

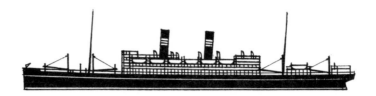

150 TENYU MARU

'08, (1908-30) 13,402. 575 x 63. Triple screw, turbines, 16 knots. Built by Mitsubishi Dockyard for Toyo Kisen Kaisha (Japan). M.V. Hong Kong, Yokohama-Honolulu, San Francisco, 2 June 1908. Transferred to Nippon Yusen Kaisha February 1926. F.V. Kobe-San Francisco, 20 March 1926. Laid up at Kobe June 1930; broken up 1933.

151 SHINYO MARU

'11, (1911-31) 13,027. Details as (150). Built by Mitsubishi Dockyard for Toyo Kisen Kaisha. M.V. Kobe-San Francisco, 26 August 1911. Transferred to NYK 1926; F.V. Kobe-San Francisco, 14 April 1926. Laid up at Kobe November 1931; broken up 1936.

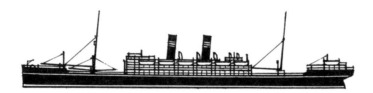

152 SIBERIA MARU

'01, (1916-30) 11,785. 572 x 63. Twin screw, quadruple expansion engines, 16 knots. Built by Newport News Shipbuilding & Drydock Co, Newport News, Va as SIBERIA for Pacific Mail Steamship Co (United States). Route: San Francisco-Hong Kong, Manila. Bought by Atlantic Transport Line (United States) 1915. Bought by Toyo Kisen Kaisha 1916; renamed SIBERIA MARU. Transferred to NYK 1926; F.V. Kobe-San Francisco, 27 April 1926. Transferred to Seattle service 1929. Laid up at Kobe 1930; broken up 1935.

153 KOREA MARU

'01, (1917-30) 11,276. Details as (152). Built by Newport News SB & D Co as KOREA for Pacific Mail. Bought by Atlantic Transport Line 1915. Bought by TKK 1916; renamed KOREA MARU. Transferred to NYK 1926; F.V. Kobe-San Francisco. 30 March 1926. Transferred to Seattle service 1930. Laid up at Kobe 1930; broken up 1934.

154 GINYO MARU
'21, (1921-43) 8,613. 445 (R) x 58. Twin screw, turbines, 12 knots. Built by Asano Shipbuilding
Co, Tsurumi for Toyo Kisen Kaisha; delivered August 1921. Route: Japan-West Coast of South
America. Transferred to NYK 1926; F.V. Yokohama-South America, 13 March 1926. Transferred
to Bombay service 1932. Returned to South American service as replacement for BOKUYO MARU;
F.V. 9 September 1939. Torpedoed and sunk by USS FLYING FISH off Taiwan, 16 December
1943.

155 BOKUYO MARU
'24, (1924-39) 8,619. Details as (154). Built by Asano Shipbuilding Co for Toyo Kisen Kaisha;
delivered October 1924. Transferred to NYK 1926. F.V. Yokohama-South America, 5 May 1926.
Sank after fire caused by heat generated in cargo of refined copper ore, 18 July 1939.

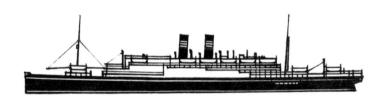

156 TAIYO MARU
'11, (1920-35) 14,458. 580 x 65. Twin screw, quadruple expansion engines, 17 knots. Built by
Blohm & Voss, Hamburg as CAP FINISTERRE for Hamburg-South American Line (Germany).
M.V. Hamburg-Rio de Janeiro, Buenos Aires, 11 November 1911. Interned in South American
waters; requisitioned as troopship by United States Government 1917. Ceded to Great Britain as
war reparation; refitted at Birkenhead 1920 and reallocated to Japan. Assigned to Toyo Kisen
Kaisha; renamed TAIYO MARU. Transferred to NYK Line 1926; F.V. Kobe-San Francisco, 31
May 1926. Transferred to Far East service 1935. Repatriated Japanese subjects from Honolulu
November 1941. Torpedoed and sunk by USS GRENADIER in China Sea, 8 May 1942.

157 ASAMA MARU
'29, (1929-44) 16,975. 583 x 72. Quadruple screw, motorship, 21 knots. Built by Mitsubishi Dockyard, Nagasaki. M.V. Yokohama-San Francisco, 10 October 1929. Repatriated Japanese subjects from Singapore and Manila, November 1941. Torpedoed and sunk by USS ATULE in South China Sea, 1 November 1944.

158 TATSUTA MARU . TATUTA MARU
'30, (1930-43) 16,975. Details as (157). Built by Mitsubishi Dockyard. M.V. Yokohama-San Francisco, 25 April 1930. Renamed TATUTA MARU 1938. Repatriated Japanese subjects from Honolulu and San Francisco October 1941; on next voyage returned to Yokohama from mid-Pacific, 8 December 1941. Torpedoed and sunk with loss of all hands by USS TARPON off Japanese coast, 8 February 1943.

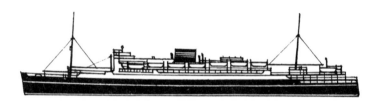

159 CHICHIBU MARU . TITIBU MARU . KAMAKURA MARU
'30, (1930-43) 17,526. 584 x 74. Twin screw, motorship, 19 knots. Built by Yokohama Dockyard, Yokohama. M.V. Yokohama-San Francisco, 4 April 1930. Renamed TITIBU MARU 1938; renamed KAMAKURA MARU January 1939. Torpedoed and sunk by USS GUDGEON in Sulu Sea while on passage from Kobe to Balikpapan, 28 April 1943.

160 HEIYO MARU
'30, (1930-43) 9,816. 482 x 60. Single screw, motorship, 17 knots. Built by Osaka Iron Works, Osaka. Replaced ANYO MARU (242) on service to West Coast of South America; M.V. Kobe-Hong Kong, South America, 19 April 1930. Torpedoed and sunk by USS WHALE northwest of Truk, 17 January 1943.

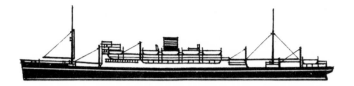

161 HIKAWA MARU

'30, (1930-60) 11,625. 536 x 66. Twin screw, motorship, 18 knots. Built by Yokohama Dock Co, Yokohama. M.V. Kobe-Seattle, 13 May 1930. Served as hospital ship in World War II; the only large Japanese passenger liner to survive the war. Returned to passenger service with reduced accommodation 1950. Laid up at Tokyo October 1960; converted to floating hostel at Yokohama 1961.

162 HIYE MARU . HIE MARU

'30, (1930-43) 11,621. Details as (161). Built by Yokohama Dock Co M.V. Kobe-Seattle, 23 August 1930. Renamed HIE MARU 1938. Repatriated Japanese subjects from Mombasa, Bombay and Rangoon, October 1941. Torpedoed and sunk by USS DRUM north of Admiralty Islands, 17 November 1943.

163 HEIAN MARU

'30, (1930-44) 11,615. Details as (161). Built by Osaka Iron Works, Osaka. M.V. Kobe-Seattle, December 1930. Served as submarine tender in war. Sunk by American carrier 'planes in Truk Lagoon, 17 February 1944.

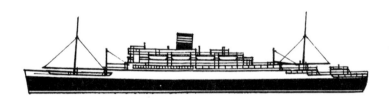

164 NITTA MARU

'40, (1940-1) 17,150. 590 x 73. Twin screw, turbines, 19 knots. Built by Mitsubishi Dockyard, Nagasaki for Japan-Europe service; transferred to transpacific trade because of war in Europe. Delivered 23 March 1940. Route: Yokohama-San Francisco, Los Angeles. The first liner with air conditioning throughout First Class passenger cabins. Set transpacific speed record, Yokohama-San Francisco, April 1941; 5490 miles in 11 days, 18 hours, 42 minutes. Transferred to Imperial Japanese Navy September 1941 for troopship service. Converted to escort aircraft carrier November 1942; renamed CHUYO. Torpedoed and sunk by USS SAILFISH off coast of Japan, 4 December 1943.

165 YAWATA MARU

'40, (1940-1) 16,500. Details as (164). Built by Mitsubishi Dockyard. Delivered 31 July 1940. Route: Yokohama-San Francisco, Los Angeles. Transferred to Navy November 1941. Commissioned as escort aircraft carrier August 1942; renamed UNYO. Torpedoed 18 January 1944; repairs completed in August. Torpedoed and sunk by USS BARB in South China Sea, 16 September 1944.

OSAKA SHOSEN KAISHA, OSAKA (1884-1964)

Founded in 1884 by a large group of Osaka Shipowners, the Osaka Shosen Kaisha (Osaka Mercantile Steamship Co) developed lines to Europe, Australia and Asiatic ports in addition to its transpacific services to Puget Sound and California, the East Coast of South America and around the world. The Company also operated over twenty Japanese coastal services.

The demand for shipping and the lack of competition in the Pacific during the First World War allowed the Line, in common with other Japanese shipping companies, to earn large profits and greatly expand its services. A number of these services were in competition with the NYK Line, and in 1931 in a deepening economic depression, the two companies arrived at an agreement which provided that NYK would discontinue its services to the East Coast of South America, while OSK would abandon its long-established route to Seattle and Tacoma.

At the outbreak of World War II the fleet comprised 46 passenger ships and nearly 90 cargo vessels. Many were of limited size, but included among them were the liners ARGENTINA MARU and BRAZIL MARU of 1939. Two additional ships, the AIKOKU MARU and HOKOKU MARU, built in 1941, were converted to auxiliary cruisers on completion.

War service resulted in the almost complete destruction of the fleet, and it was not until the early 1950s that the Company returned to the transpacific trade with the emigrant ships AMERICA MARU, AFRICA MARU and SANTOS MARU. These were followed by a second BRAZIL MARU and ARGENTINA MARU in 1954 and 1958.

In 1964 the Company joined with Mitsui Sempaku Shosen to form Mitsui-OSK Lines.

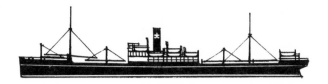

166 HAWAII MARU
'15, (1915-44) 9,482. 475 (R) x 61. Twin screw, triple expansion engines, 13 knots. Built by Mitsubishi Dockyard, Nagasaki; delivered 27 July 1915. Route: Hong Kong, Kobe- Seattle, Tacoma. Transferred to South American service August 1925-June 1930. Sold to Nanyo Kaiun Kaisha February 1943. Torpedoed and sunk by USS SEA DEVIL in East China Sea, 2 December 1944.

167 MANILA MARU
'15, (1915-44) 9,486. Details as (166). Built by Mitsubishi Dockyard; delivered 4 September 1915. Route: Japan-Puget Sound: transferred to South America service December 1923-November 1929. Torpedoed and sunk by USS MINGO off coast of Sarawak, 25 November 1944.

168 AFRICA MARU
'18, (1918-42) 9,475. Details as (166). Built by Mitsubishi Dockyard; delivered 28 February 1918. Route: Japan-Puget Sound; transferred to South America service June 1931-September 1941. Torpedoed and sunk by USS FINBACK in Formosa Strait, 20 October 1942.

169 ARABIA MARU
'18, (1918-44) 9,480. Details as (166). Built by Mitsubishi Dockyard; delivered 30 April 1918. Route: Japan-Puget Sound. Made last OSK sailing from Seattle July 1931; transferred to South American service until September 1941. Torpedoed and sunk by USS BLUEGILL off Luzon, 18 October 1944.

170 ARIZONA MARU
'20, (1920-42) 9,684. Details as (166). Built by Mitsubishi Dockyard; delivered 20 June 1920. Route: Japan-Puget Sound; transferred to South American service September 1931-October 1938. Sunk by American carrier planes north of Guadalcanal, 14 November 1942.

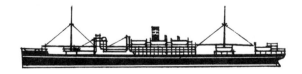

171 SANTOS MARU
'25, (1925-44) 7,266. 430 (R) x 56. Twin screw, motorship, 15 knots. 38 First Class passengers. Built by Mitsubishi Dockyard, Nagasaki; delivered November 1925. The first passenger motorship built in Japan. Route: Westbound round-the-world via Hong Kong, Singapore, Colombo, South African and South American ports, New Orleans, Galveston and Los Angeles. Discontinued service April 1940. Converted to submarine tender 1941; later served as transport. Torpedoed and sunk by USS ATULE in Sulu Sea, 25 November 1944.

172 LA PLATA MARU
'26, (1926-45) 7,267. Details as (171). Built by Mitsubishi Dockyard. M.V. Japan-South Africa, South America, May 1926. Dicsontinued service February 1940. Renamed KANJU MARU 1941. Sunk by air attack in Saigon harbour January 1945.

173 MONTEVIDEO MARU
'26, (1926-42) 7,267. Details as (171). Built by Mitsubishi Dockyard. M.V. Japan-South Africa, South America, August 1926. Final voyage September 1941. Torpedoed and sunk by USS STURGEON in South China Sea, 1 July 1942.

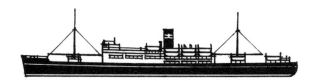

174 BUENOS AIRES MARU
'29, (1929-43) 9,626. 473 x 62. Twin screw, motorship, 17 knots. Built by Mitsubishi Dockyard; delivered 31 October 1929. Route: Japan-Westbound round-the-world via South Africa and South America. Final voyage October 1941. Sunk by American planes 27 November 1943.

175 RIO DE JANEIRO MARU
'30, (1930-44) 9,627. Details as (174)..Built by Mitsubishi Dockyard; delivered 15 May 1930. Route: Japan-South Africa, South America. Discontinued service October 1940. Converted to submarine tender 1941; later served as transport. Sunk by American air attack, 17 February 1944.

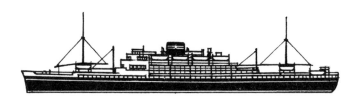

176 ARGENTINA MARU
'39, (1939-43) 12,755. 544 x 68. Twin screw, motorship, 21.5 knots. Built by Mitsubishi Dockyard, Nagasaki; delivered 31 May 1939. Route: Westbound round-the-world via South African and South American ports. Converted to troopship May 1942. Commissioned as escort aircraft carrier November 1943; renamed KAIYO. Torpedoed 24 July 1945; damaged by bombs four days later. Ran aground and capsized outside Beppu harbour; broken up 1946.

177 BRAZIL MARU
'39, (1940-2) 12,752. Details as (176). Built by Mitsubishi Dockyard; delivered 23 December 1939. Route: Japan-South Africa, South America. Torpedoed and sunk by USS GREENLING north-east of Truk, 5 August 1942.

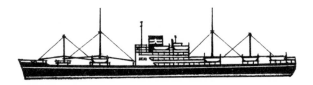

178 AMERICA MARU

'50, (1951-64) 8,343. 473 x 62. Single screw, motorship, 14 knots. Built by Central Japan Heavy Industries, Kobe as cargo ship; delivered 25 December 1950. Emigrant accommodation added after completion. Route: Japan-East Coast of South America. Sold to Nippon Ijusen Kaisha September 1963. Transferred to Mitsui-OSK Lines 1964. Passenger accommodation reduced to twelve same year. Sold to State Shipping Co (Panama) 1967; renamed VANKOWA. Renamed VANMINT 1968.

179 AFRICA MARU

'51, (1951-65) 8,354. Details as (178). Built by Central Japan Heavy Industries; delivered 17 March 1951. Sold to Nippon Ijusen Kaisha 1963. Transferred to Mitsui-OSK Lines 1964. Passenger accommodation reduced to twelve 1965. Sold to Marlene Shipping Co (Panama) 1967; renamed VANLENE. Went aground at entrance to Barkley Sound, Vancouver Island, 14 March 1972, became a total loss.

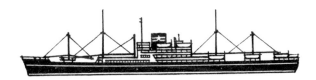

180 SANTOS MARU

'52, (1952-65) 8,516. 475 x 62. Single screw, motorship, 14.5 knots. Built by Shin Mitsubishi Heavy Industries, Kobe as cargo ship; delivered 10 December 1952. Emigrant accommodation added after completion. Sold to Nippon Ijusen Kaisha 1963. Transferred to Mitsui-OSK Lines 1964. Passenger accommodation reduced to twelve 1965. Sold to Liberty Maritime Corp (Panama) 1972; renamed WINONA.

G

MITSUI-O.S.K. LINES, TOKYO (1964-   )

The Mitsui-OSK Lines Ltd was formed 1 April 1964 by the amalgamation of the Osaka Shosen Kaisha and Mitsui Kinkai Kisen Sempaku Kaisha to form a joint fleet totaling over 2,300,000 gross tons of shipping. It thus became the largest shipping firm in Japan and second in the world only to the P & O Group.

Soon afterward the OSK emigrant ships AMERICA MARU, AFRICA MARU and SANTOS MARU had their passenger accommodation reduced to 12, while the Line's two largest ships, the ARGENTINA MARU and BRAZIL MARU were refitted for regular passenger service to the east coast of South America via California and the Panama Canal. The SAKURA MARU, owned by Nihon Sangyo Junko Mihonichi Kyokai was continued under the Line's operation in her dual role as passenger liner and exhibit ship for the Japan Industry Floating Fair Association.

Early in 1972 the SAKURA MARU was sold and the ARGENTINA MARU was withdrawn and refitted as the cruise ship NIPPON MARU. The South American service was thus reduced to the sailings of the BRAZIL MARU which were scheduled to end in 1973.

98

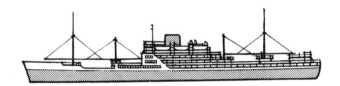

181 BRAZIL MARU
'54, (1954-   ) 10,216. 512 x 64. Single screw, motorship, 16 knots. Built by Mitsubishi Heavy
Industries, Kobe as emigrant ship for Osaka Shosen Kaisha; delivered 10 July 1954. Route:
Yokohama, Kobe-Honolulu, San Francisco, Los Angeles and East Coast of South America.
Transferred to Mitsui-OSK Lines 1964; refitted for economy class passenger service August 1965.
Scheduled to be withdrawn from service 1973.

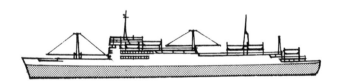

182 ARGENTINA MARU
'58, (1958-72) 10,908. 513 x 67. Single screw, turbines, 16.5 knots. Built by Mitsubishi Heavy
Industries as emigrant ship for Osaka Shosen Kaisha. M.V. Yokohama-South America 2 June 1958.
Transferred to Mitsui-OSK Lines 1964; refitted for passenger service October 1965. Withdrawn
from transpacific service February 1972 and refitted as cruise ship; renamed NIPPON MARU.

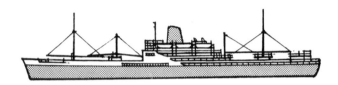

183 SAKURA MARU
'62, (1965-72) 12,628. 515 x 69. Single screw, motorship, 17 knots. Built by Mitsubishi Heavy
Industries; delivered 15 October 1962. Designed primarily as floating fair and exhibition ship for
Japan Industrial Trade Fair Assoc Operated as passenger ship periodically after 1965 by Mitsui-
OSK Lines on Japan-East Coast of South America service. Sold to Oshima Unyu Kaisha (Japan)
1972; renamed SAKURA.

6 FRANCE

MESSAGERIES MARITIMES, MARSEILLES (1923-71)

In 1861 the Cie des Services Maritimes des Messageries Imperiales, which had been operating mail shipping services in the Mediterranean and to South America, received a mail contract for service to India and the Far East. Sailings were begun in October of the following year when the steamer NEVA left Marseilles to connect with the IMPERATRICE at Suez. As sailings on the route increased in frequency, the Company became a formidable competitor of the British P & O.

After the downfall of the monarchy in 1871, the Company name was changed to the Cie des Messageries Maritimes. Ten years later a service was begun to Australia and New Caledonia via Reunion and Mauritius.

The advent of World War I saw the disruption of trade and such severe losses to the fleet that despite the use of ex-German vessels, service was slow in returning to normal. In 1923 the sister ships EL KANTARA and LOUQSOR were switched to a new Pacific route via the Panama Canal to Tahiti and Noumea. They were followed soon afterward by the ANTINOUS.

Heavy shipping losses were again sustained in the Second World War, and it was not until 1952 that two new ships, the CALEDONIEN and TAHITIEN, entered the Pacific service. In 1958 the Costa Line's BIANCA C. was chartered and renamed MELANESIEN, but five years later she was replaced by another chartered vessel the OCEANIEN, formerly the Holland-America Line's NOORDAM. The OCEANIEN was sold in turn for breaking up in 1967. Late in 1971 the CALEDONIEN and TAHITIEN were withdrawn and the service was continued with fast cargo liners of limited passenger capacity.

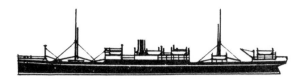

184 LOUQSOR

'04, (1923-30) 6,889. 464 x 53. Twin screw, triple expansion engines, 12 knots. Built by Messageries Maritimes, La Ciotat. Route: Marseilles-Far East. Resumed post-war passenger service from Marseilles to Colombo, Sydney and Noumea 1920. Transferred to Tahiti, Noumea service via Panama Canal, March 1923. Broken up Belgium 1930.

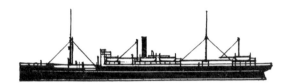

185 ANTINOUS

'13, (1923-31) 7,133. 445 x 56. Single screw, triple expansion engines, 11 knots. Built by Flensburger Schiffsbau, Flensburg as WACHTFELS for Hansa Line (Germany). Converted to auxiliary cruiser WOLF 1916; operated for fifteen months as mine-layer and commerce raider in Indian Ocean and South Pacific. Ceded to French Government as war reparation.1919. Bought by Messageries Maritimes 1923; renamed ANTINOUS. Route: Marseilles-Noumea via Suez. Transferred to Panama Canal route; F.V. Marseilles-Tahiti, Noumea, 17 July 1923. Broken up Genoa 1931.

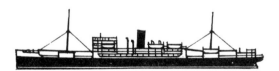

186 VILLE DE STRASBOURG

'20, (1935-52) 7,138. 425 x 53. Single screw, triple expansion engines, 13 knots. Built by North of Ireland Shipbuilding Co, Londonderry for Cie Havraise Peninsulaire (France). Chartered by Messageries Maritimes; F.V. Marseilles-Colombo, Sydney and Noumea, 9 September 1922. Purchased 1928; accommodation enlarged. Transferred to Marseilles-Tahiti, Noumea service via Panama 1935. Captured by British forces in Indian Ocean, March 1941; operated as troopship by Ministry of War Transport under Union-Castle Line management. Resumed passenger service 10 September 1945. Broken up Faslane 1952.

187 VILLE D'AMIENS

'24, (1935-53) 7,143. Details as (186). Built by North of Ireland Shipbuilding Co for Cie Havraise Peninsulaire. Chartered by Messageries Maritimes upon completion; F.V. Marseilles-Colombo, Sydney and Noumea, 10 March 1925. Purchased and refitted 1928. Transferred to Panama Canal route 1935. Taken over by British at Papeete July 1940; operated as troopship under Clan Line management. Resumed passenger service 29 October 1945. Broken up La Seyne 1953.

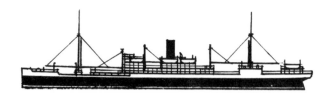

188 COMMISSAIRE RAMEL

'20, (1935-40) 10,061. 499 x 59. Single screw, triple expansion engines, 13 knots. Built by Soc Provencale de Construction Navale, La Ciotat as cargo vessel; refitted with passenger accommodation 1926. F.V. Marseilles-Colombo, Sydney and Noumea, 19 January 1927. Transferred to Panama Canal route; F.V. Marseilles-Tahiti, Noumea, 8 April 1935. Taken over by British forces after fall of France July 1940. Sunk by German raider TAMESIS in Indian Ocean, 17 September 1940.

189 SAGITTAIRE

'29, (1939-54) 8,254. 494 x 61. Twin screw, motorship, 14.5 knots. Built by Bremer Vulkan, Vegesack as cargo liner WASHINGTON for Cie Générale Transatlantique (France). Route: Northern Europe-Pacific Coast of North America. Transferred to Messageries Maritimes September 1938; renamed SAGITTAIRE and refitted as passenger vessel. F.V. Marseilles-Tahiti, Noumea, 19 March 1939. On colonial service under French control throughout World War II; reopened passenger service March 1944. Sold to Maritima Asiatic Panamense (Panama) May 1954; renamed PACIFIC GLORY. Sold to Pacific Bulk Carriers (Panama) 1956; renamed OCEANIC RELIANCE. Broken up Mihara, Japan 1959.

190 CALEDONIEN
'52, (1952-71) 12,712. 549 x 68. Twin screw, motorship, 16 knots. Built by Soc des Ateliers et Chantiers de France, Dunkirk. M.V. Marseilles-Tahiti, Noumea and Sydney, 1 October 1952. Laid up at Marseilles November 1971. Sold to Island of Cyprus Shipping Co (Panama) March 1972; renamed NISOS-KYPROS.

191 TAHITIEN
'53, (1953-71) 12,614. Details as (190). Built by Naval Dockyard, Brest. M.V. Marseilles-Tahiti, Noumea and Sydney, 4 May 1953. Damaged by engine room fire in Pacific on voyage from Marseilles to Sydney, 12 May 1969. Towed to Balboa by cargo liner MARQUISIEN; later towed to Marseilles for repairs. Sold to Aphrodite Cruises (Cyprus) 1971; renamed ATALANTE.

192 MELANESIEN
'25, (1958-63) 9,905. 507 x 60. Twin screw, motorship, 15 knots. Built by De Schelde, Flushing as INDRAPOERA for Royal Rotterdam Lloyd; the first large Dutch motor passenger ship. Route: Rotterdam-Dutch East Indies. Lengthened 1932 and again in 1934 after fire at Southampton. Bought by Providencia Shipping Co (Panama) 1956; renamed ASUNCION. Bought by Costa Line (Italy) 1957; renamed BIANCA C. Chartered by Messageries Maritimes 1958; renamed MELANESIEN. Broken up Genoa 1963.

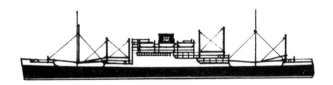

193 OCEANIEN·
'38, (1963-7) 9,763. 502 x 64. Twin screw, motorship, 17 knots. Built by P. Smit Jr, Rotterdam as NOORDAM for Holland-America Line (Netherlands). Served as Allied troopship 1942-6. Bought by Cielomar Steamship Corp (Panama) 1963; chartered by Messageries Maritimes and renamed OCEANIEN. F.V. Marseilles-Tahiti, Noumea and Sydney, 2 August 1963. Broken up Split 1967.

7 NETHERLANDS

ROYAL ROTTERDAM LLOYD, ROTTERDAM (1959-64)

The Koninklijke Rotterdam Lloyd had its origin in 1844 when Willem Ruys of Rotterdam sent a small sailing ship to Java. Shipping operations were expanded over the years under the firm of Wm Ruys & Zonen, and in 1883 a royal charter was granted.

The Line's extensive Far East mail and cargo services were completely disrupted by the outbreak of World War II and three of its passenger vessels, the BALOERAN, DEMPO and SLAMAT, were lost to enemy action. The Company's largest liner, the WILLEM RUYS, laid down before the war, remained unfinished for nearly nine years.

With the independence of Indonesia in 1949 the Far East trade steadily diminished, and the liners INDRAPOERA and SIBAJAK were withdrawn and eventually sold. The WILLEM RUYS was transferred in 1959 to a new round-the-world service, but due to declining revenues, was laid up late in 1964 and sold the next year.

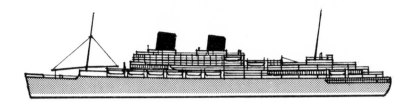

194 WILLEM RUYS
'47, (1959-64) 23,114. 631 x 82. Twin screw, motorship, 21 knots. Laid down January 1939 by De Schelde, Flushing. Lay in stocks throughout World War II; completed late 1947. M.V. Rotterdam-Indonesia, December 1947. Chartered to Europe-Canada Line for two transatlantic voyages 1958. Refitted at Schiedam 1958-9; transferred to eastbound round-the-world service from Rotterdam March 1959. Sold to Flotta Lauro January 1965; renamed ACHILLE LAURO (209).

NEDERLAND LINE, AMSTERDAM (1959-64)

The Stoomvaart Maatschappij 'Nederland' was founded in 1870 to establish a shipping service between Holland and the East Indies via the Suez Canal which had been opened the previous year. Four ships were ordered and the first, the WILLEM III, left Den Helder for Batavia on 18 May 1871 only to be abandoned when she caught fire off Portsmouth the next day. The Company prospered, however, and by 1882 a ship was leaving Amsterdam every ten days. Five years later a joint weekly service was established with Rotterdam Lloyd.

A limited service was maintained throughout World War I, but in the Second World War Holland was invaded at a time when three of the Company's six passenger ships were in Dutch ports. Two escaped, but the JAN PIETERZOON COEN was scuttled at Ijmuiden and in the course of the war two more ships were lost.

In 1957 the Indonesian Government began expropriating Dutch property and the East Indies trade came to an end. The Line's two remaining passenger ships, the JOHAN VAN OLDENBARNEVELT and ORANJE, were put on a round-the-world service but in 1963-4 both were sold and the service was discontinued.

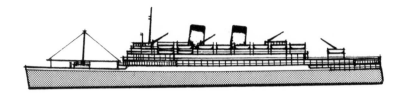

195   JOHAN VAN OLDENBARNEVELT

'30, (1959-63) 20,314. 609 x 75. Twin screw, motorship, 17 knots. Built by Nederlandsche
Scheepsbouw Maatschappij, Amsterdam. Route: Amsterdam-Batavia. M.V. delayed by collision
with Dutch steamer REGGESTROOM in North Sea Canal, 7 May 1930. Served as Allied troopship
in World War II. Chartered by Dutch Government for Australian emigrant service 1950. F.V.
Amsterdam-Fremantle, Melbourne and Sydney, 2 September 1950. Extensively remodelled at
Amsterdam 1958-9; transferred to eastbound round-the-world service. Sold to Greek Line
(Greece) March 1963; renamed LAKONIA. Caught fire while on cruise from Southampton and
abandoned with loss of 128 lives, 22 December 1963. Capsized and sank 250 miles west of
Gibraltar while under tow seven days later.

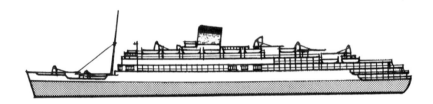

196   ORANJE

'39, (1959-64) 20,565. 656 x 83. Triple screw, motorship, 21.5 knots. Built by Nederlandsche
Scheepsbouw Maats. M.V. Amsterdam-Djakarta July 1939. Laid up at Soerabaya December 1939.
Converted to hospital ship for Australian Government at Sydney 1941. Resumed passenger
service to East Indies July 1946; transferred to Australian emigrant trade 1950. Refitted at
Amsterdam; placed on westbound round-the-world service 1959. Sold to Flotta Lauro September
1964; renamed ANGELINA LAURO (208).

ROYAL INTEROCEAN LINES, AMSTERDAM. HONG KONG (1960-   )

The Koninklijke Java-China Paketvaart Linjen N.V., popularly known as the Royal Interocean Lines, was formed in 1947 by the amalgamation of the Java-China-Japan Lijn and a portion of the Koninklijke Paketvaart Maatschappij.

The Java-China-Japan Line had been founded in 1903 to connect the principal islands of the Dutch East Indies with Chinese and Japanese ports, while the KPM or Royal Packet Navigation Co, began service in 1891 with a fleet of vessels sailing in inter-island services throughout the wide expanse of the East Indies. The KPM fleet eventually grew to number about 150 ships, mostly of small size, but including the NIEUW HOLLAND and NIEUW ZEELAND of 1927 and the large motorships BOISSEVAIN, RUYS and TEGELBERG built in 1931. They sailed on a network of no less than 68 regular shipping lines.

After the losses and disruptions of World War II, the two companies combined forces, and nine KPM passenger vessels were added to the fleet of the Java-China-Japan Line which included the liners TJITJALENGKA, TJISADANE and TJINEGARA. The larger ships of the combined fleet sailed on a Far East-Africa-South America service.

In 1960 two post-war motorships, the TJILUWAH and TJIWANGI, began a new service between Australia, Hong Kong and Japan. The TJILUWAH was sold early in 1972 and was replaced by the purchase of the Holland-Africa Line's RANDFONTEIN which entered Pacific service as the second NIEUW HOLLAND.

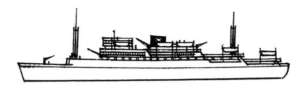

197   TJIWANGI

'50, (1960-   ) 9,092. 479 x 63. Single screw, motorship, 14 knots. Built by C. van der Giessen &
Zonen, Krimpen. Route: Hong Kong – Dutch East Indies. Transferred to Australia-Japan, Hong
Kong service; F.V. Melbourne, Sydney, Brisbane-Yokkaichi, Yokohama, 29 July 1960.

198   TJILUWAH

'51, (1960-72) 9,849. Details as (197). Built by C. van der Giessen. F.V. Australia-Japan, 29
August 1960. Sold to Pacific International Lines (Singapore) January 1972; renamed KOTA
SINGAPURA.

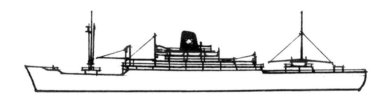

199   NIEUW HOLLAND

'58, (1972-   ) 13,694. 585 x 70. Twin screw, motorship, 18 knots. Built by Wilton-Fijenoord,
Schiedam as RANDFONTEIN for Holland-Africa Line of United Netherlands Navigation Co.
(Netherlands). M.V. Amsterdam-South and East Africa, January 1959. Transferred to Koninklijke
Nedlloyd 1970. Bought by Royal Interocean Lines 1971; renamed NIEUW HOLLAND. F.V. Hong
Kong-Australia, 21 January 1972.

8 ITALY

COGEDAR LINE, GENOA (1963-8)

In 1954 the Compania Genovese d'Armamento, commonly known as the Cogedar Line, purchased the 26-year-old Canadian Pacific cargo ship BEAVERBRAE and renamed her AURELIA. She was fitted with air-conditioned accommodation for over 1100 tourist class passengers and placed on a Genoa-Australia emigrant service. Soon afterward another ageing cargo vessel, the GENOVA, was renamed FLAMINIA and similarly refitted.

Five years later the Cunard Line's transatlantic liner MEDIA was acquired, renamed FLAVIA and extensively remodelled with accommodation increased to provide for 1220 passengers. In 1963 she was diverted to a round-the-world service from Rotterdam via Panama in which she was joined by the AURELIA a year later.

The AURELIA returned to the Australian trade after three voyages and the FLAVIA was sold in 1968 to end the Company's Pacific services.

200 AURELIA

'38, (1964-5) 10,480. 487 x 60. Single screw, diesel-electric. 17 knots. Built by Blohm & Voss, Hamburg as cargo ship HUASCARAN for Hamburg American Line (Germany). Ceded to Canadian Government as war reparation 1945. Bought by Canadian Pacific and refitted to carry westbound emigrants 1947; renamed BEAVERBRAE. Bought by Cogedar Line November 1954; renamed AURELIA and refitted for passenger service at Monfalcone. F.V. Trieste-Sydney, 13 May 1955. Service extended to northern European ports 1959. F.V. from Rotterdam and Southampton westbound round-the-world via Panama, 9 December 1964. Reverted to Australian trade after three voyages. Sold to Chandris Line for cruising service 1970; renamed ROMANZA.

201 FLAVIA

'47, (1963-8) 15,465. 556 x 70. Twin screw, turbines, 18 knots. Built by John Brown & Co, Clydebank, Glasgow as MEDIA for Cunard Line (Great Britain). M.V. Liverpool-New York, 20 August 1947. Bought by Cogedar Line October 1961; renamed FLAVIA and extensively refitted with increased accommodation at Genoa 1961-2. F.V. Genoa-Fremantle, Melbourne and Sydney, September 1962. Transferred to westbound round-the-world service from Rotterdam and Southampton 1963. Sold to Costa Line (Italy) for cruising service 1968.

SITMAR LINE, GENOA (1957-   )

The Società Italiana Trasporti Marittima, founded in 1938 as a tramp shipping firm, prepared to enter the emigrant trade with the purchase in 1949 of the British India liner KENYA, then laid up after war service as a landing ship. A second ship, the American escort aircraft carrier USS CHARGER, was also acquired, renamed FAIRSEA and refitted with accommodation for 1,800 passengers. The KENYA, after a two year delay, was renamed CASTEL FELICE and similarly converted. Both ships were sailed on a variety of services from the North Atlantic to Central America and Australia.

Another former aircraft carrier, rebuilt as the cargo ship CASTEL FORTE in 1952, was refitted to carry emigrant passengers in 1957 and renamed FAIRSKY, to enter the Australian service the following year. Similarly in 1963 the Bibby Line troopship OXFORDSHIRE, laid up following the premature termination of her trooping contract, was purchased and renamed FAIRSTAR. After extensive refit she sailed for Australian ports in May 1964.

Beginning in 1957 homeward voyages were occasionally taken by way of the Panama Canal and in later years the Pacific route was followed on most sailings. On one of these in 1969 the FAIRSEA caught fire in mid-Pacific and though towed to port, was sold for breaking up. The next year the forty-year-old CASTEL FELICE was also retired.

Late in 1968 the Company bought the Cunard transatlantic liners CARINTHIA and SYLVANIA and after a two year delay, extensively refitted them as the FAIRSEA and FAIRWIND for cruising service in tropical waters.

112

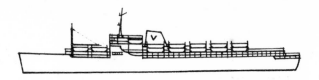

202 FAIRSEA

'41, (1957-69) 13,317. 492 x 70. Single screw, motorship, 16 knots. Launched by Sun Shipbuilding & Drydock Co, Chester, Penna. as cargo liner RIO DE LA PLATA for Moore-McCormack Line (United States). Completed as escort aircraft carrier USS CHARGER (CVE-30). Bought by Sitmar Line 1949; renamed FAIRSEA. Registered in Panama; refitted as emigrant carrier 1949-50. Chartered by Australian Government for emigrant service 1955. F.V. Southampton-Melbourne, Sydney, 6 December 1955. Occasional homeward voyages via Panama Canal after February 1957. Registry transferred to Italy 1958; reverted to Panama 1968. Disabled by fire in engine room 900 miles west of Panama, 24 January 1969. Towed to Balboa by American freighter LOUISE LYKES; broken up La Spezia.

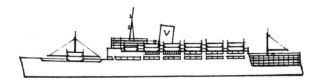

203 CASTEL FELICE

'30, (1957-70) 10,953. 493 x 64. Twin screw, turbines, 16 knots. Built by Alexander Stephen & Sons, Linthouse, Glasgow as KENYA for British India Steam Navigation Co (Great Britain). Converted to infantry landing ship 1940; renamed HMS KEREN. Bought by subsidiary of Sitmar Line 1949; registered in Panama and renamed KENYA, KEREN and FAIRSTONE while laid up in Holy Loch. Towed to Genoa and refitted 1951-2; renamed CASTEL FELICE. Registered in Italy and placed on Italy-South America service. Transferred to North Atlantic 1954 and to Australia-New Zealand service 1956; inaugurated homeward route via Panama January 1957. Registry transferred to Panama 1968. Broken up Kaohsiung 1970.

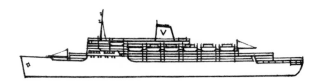

204 FAIRSKY

'42, (1966-72) 12,464. 492 x 70. Single screw, turbines, 17 knots. Laid down by Western Pipe & Steel Co, San Francisco as cargo liner STEEL ARTISAN; completed as escort aircraft carrier USS BARNES. Transferred to Royal Navy 1942; renamed HMS ATTACKER. Returned to US Navy 1946. Bought by Sitmar Line 1952; rebuilt as cargo ship. Renamed CASTEL FORTE and registered in Panama. Refitted as passenger ship at New York and Genoa 1957-8; renamed FAIRSKY. F.V. Southampton-Australia, 26 June 1958. Registry transferred to Liberia 1966. Route: Southampton-Eastbound round-the-world. Laid up at Genoa 1972.

H

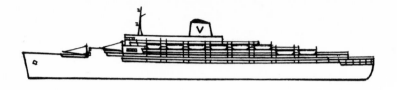

205 FAIRSTAR

'57, (1966-   ) 23,764. 609 x 78. Twin screw, turbines, 17 knots. Built by Fairfield Shipbuilding &
Engineering Co, Govan, Glasgow as troopship OXFORDSHIRE for Bibby Line (Great Britain).
Government trooping charter cancelled December 1962; laid up at Falmouth. Bought by Sitmar
Line and refitted at Schiedam 1963-4; renamed FAIRSTAR and registered in Liberia. F.V.
Southampton-Australia, 19 May 1964; alternate homeward voyages via Panama.

LLOYD TRIESTINO, TRIESTE (1971-   )

When Trieste was ceded to Italy after the First World War, the 83-year-old Lloyd Austriaco, which had achieved a leading position in the Far East trade, was reconstituted as the Soc di Navigazione Lloyd Triestino. In the years prior to World War II a large fleet was built up under government subsidy.

The end of the war found the Company in a state of complete collapse, and for the next few years services were irregular at best. In 1951 however, three new ships, the AUSTRALIA, OCEANIA and NEPTUNIA entered service on a route from Genoa to Australia, followed the next year by the AFRICA and EUROPA on the East African service, and the VICTORIA and ASIA on the Far East trade.

In 1963 the Line's largest and fastest ships, the GALILEO GALILEI and GUGLIELMO MARCONI, were built for the Australian service, allowing the three earlier ships to be transferred to the Italian Line's service to the West Coast of South America. In June of 1971 the GALILEO GALILEI continued eastward across the Pacific on the first of a series of round-the-world voyages.

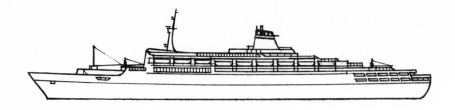

206   GALILEO GALILEI
'63, (1971-   ) 27, 888. 702 x 94. Twin screw, turbines, 24 knots. Built by Cantieri Riuniti dell'
Adriatico, Monfalcone. M.V. Genoa-Fremantle, Melbourne and Sydney, 22 April 1963. Sailed on
first eastbound round-the-world voyage from Genoa, 1 June 1971.

207   GUGLIELMO MARCONI
'63, (1972-   ) 27,905. Details as (206). Built by Cantieri Riuniti dell' Adriatico. M.V. Genoa-
Australia, 18 November 1963. Continued voyage across Pacific from Brisbane, 17 June 1972.

FLOTTA LAURO, NAPLES (1968-   )

The Flotta Lauro was founded by Achille Lauro in 1923 to engage in tramping and in trade between Italy and East Africa. Soon after the end of World War II the Company bought three surplus American naval vessels and refitted them for passenger service. One, the former Grace liner SANTA MARIA, was renamed SURRIENTO and placed in a service to Central America, while the other two, as the ROMA and SYDNEY, entered the Italy-Australia trade.

In 1964-5 two Dutch liners, the WILLEM RUYS and ORANJE, were purchased, renamed ACHILLE LAURO and ANGELINA LAURO, and extensively rebuilt for the Australian service. Late in 1968 the ANGELINA LAURO inaugurated a homeward route from New Zealand via the Straits of Magellan.

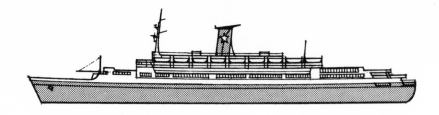

208   ANGELINA LAURO
'39, (1968-   ) 24,377. 672 x 83. Formerly ORANJE (196) Nederland Line. Bought by Flotta
Lauro September 1964; renamed ANGELINA LAURO. Extensively rebuilt at Genoa; work
delayed by fire in yard 24 August 1965. F.V. Bremerhaven-Sydney, Wellington, 6 March 1966.
First homeward voyage from Sydney via Straits of Magellan, 28 September 1968. Transferred to
Caribbean cruising service November 1972.

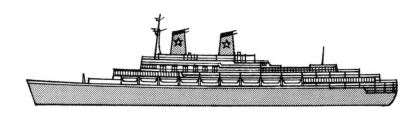

209   ACHILLE LAURO
'47, (1969-   ) 23,629. Formerly WILLEM RUYS (194) Royal Rotterdam Lloyd. Bought by
Flotta Lauro January 1965; renamed ACHILLE LAURO. Extensively refitted at Palermo; work
delayed by fire in yard 29 August 1965. F.V. Genoa-Sydney, Wellington, 13 April 1966. First
homeward voyage from Sydney via Straits of Magellan, 27 January 1969. Damaged by fire while
undergoing refit at Genoa, 19 May 1972; out of service nearly five months.

9 GREECE

CHANDRIS LINES, PIRAEUS (1964-   )

In 1959 the firm of D & A Chandris embarked on a programme of buying ships and refitting them for Mediterranean cruising as well as for emigrant service to Australia. The Union-Castle liner BLOEMFONTEIN CASTLE was purchased and renamed PATRIS, and after a refit, sailed from Piraeus in December 1959. A second ship, the BRETAGNE of the Soc Générale de Transports Maritimes, was chartered in 1961 and renamed BRITTANY. She became a total loss after a fire in the yard at Skaramanga two years later.

As a replacement, the Matson Lines' LURLINE, now 31 years old, was purchased, renamed ELLINIS and extensively rebuilt for the Australian service. After her first voyage she was routed homeward via the Panama Canal. The venture proved successful and another American liner, the United States Line's AMERICA, was acquired as a running mate. Renamed AUSTRALIS, she was refitted in 1965 with greatly increased capacity.

In 1970 the Company bought a second LURLINE, built in 1932 as the MONTEREY. Given a similar reconditioning, she entered the round-the-world service from Southampton early in 1971 as the BRITANIS.

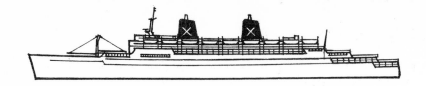

210 ELLINIS

'32, (1964-) 24, 251. 642 x 79. Formerly LURLINE (98) Matson Lines. Bought by Chandris Lines 1963; renamed ELLINIS, and extensively refitted at Piraeus. F.V. Piraeus-Melbourne, Sydney, 30 December 1963. Homeward voyages routed alternately via Panama to Southampton 1964.

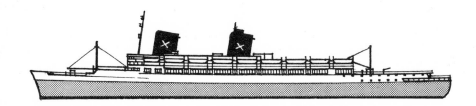

211 AUSTRALIS

'40, (1965-) 34,449. 723 x 93. Twin screw, turbines, 23 knots. Built by Newport News Shipbuilding & Drydock Co, Newport News, Va as AMERICA for United States Lines (United States). M.V. New York-West Indies, 10 August 1940. Commissioned as US Navy transport 1942; renamed USS WEST POINT (AP-23). Refitted at Newport News; renamed AMERICA and returned to passenger service. F.V. New York-Cobh, Southampton and Le Havre, 14 November 1946. Bought by Chandris Lines 1964; renamed AUSTRALIS. Accommodation enlarged at Piraeus. F.V. Piraeus-Melbourne, Sydney, 20 August 1965. Alternate homeward voyages taken via Panama after October 1965. Registry transferred to Panama 1969.

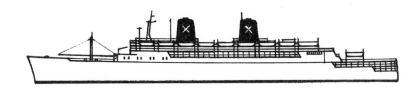

212 BRITANIS

'32, (1971-) 24,351. Formerly LURLINE (99) Matson Lines. Bought by Chandris Lines 1970; renamed BRITANIS and refitted at Piraeus. F.V. Southampton-Eastbound round-the-world, 21 February 1971.

10 TAIWAN

ORIENT OVERSEAS LINE, TAIPEI (1965-   )

The Chinese Maritime Trust Ltd of Taiwan, headed by C.Y. Tung, began a trans-pacific passenger service in 1965 with the purchase of two American Export Isbrandtsen liners, the EXCALIBUR and EXOCHORDA. Renamed ORIENTAL JADE and ORIENTAL PEARL, they were placed on a service between Hong Kong, Taiwan and California ports under the operation of the Orient Overseas Line.

In 1966 six nearly identical West German ships, three each from the Hamburg American Line and Norddeutscher Lloyd, were acquired. They were all given 'Oriental' names and operated on a route which extended to Gulf and East Coast ports of the United States.

In the next three years, the Company added three New Zealand Shipping Co liners, the RUAHINE, RANGITANE and RANGITOTO, which were renamed ORIENTAL RIO, ORIENTAL ESMERALDA and ORIENTAL CARNAVEL respectively and placed on a new round-the-world service. At the same time two Holland-America Line ships, the DIEMERDYK and DINTELDYK, were acquired and renamed ORIENTAL AMIGA and ORIENTAL FANTASIA to join the Pacific-East Coast service. All the Line's passenger ships except the ORIENTAL RIO were registered in Liberia.

In 1970 the former Cunard liner Queen Elizabeth, lying in Fort Lauderdale, Florida as an exhibit and convention centre, was purchased, renamed SEAWISE UNIVERSITY, and sailed to Hong Kong for conversion to a cruise ship and floating university. Soon afterward the American Export Isbrandtsen's ATLANTIC which had been laid up at Baltimore was also acquired, renamed UNIVERSE CAMPUS, and refitted for the same service. The SEAWISE UNIVERSITY, with her refit nearly completed, caught fire January 1972, capsized and became a total loss.

I

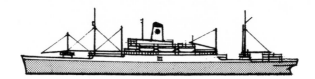

213 ORIENTAL JADE

'44, (1965-   ) 9,645. 473 x 66. Single screw, turbines, 18 knots. 124 passengers. Built by
Bethlehem Steel Corp, Sparrows Point, Maryland as US Navy attack transport USS DUTCHESS
(APA-98). Bought by American Export Line (United States) 1948; renamed EXCALIBUR. F.V.
New York-Mediterranean, 24 September 1948. Bought by Orient Overseas Line 1965; renamed
ORIENTAL JADE. F.V. San Francisco-Yokohama, 29 December 1965. Route: Hong Kong,
Taiwan, Japan-San Francisco, Los Angeles and San Diego.

214 ORIENTAL PEARL

'45, (1966-   ) 9,645. Details as (213). Built by Bethlehem Steel Corp as USS SHELBY (APA-105).
Bought by American Export Line 1948; renamed EXETER. F.V. New York-Mediterranean, 1
December 1948. Bought by Orient Overseas Line 1965; renamed ORIENTAL PEARL. F.V. San
Francisco-Yokohama, 18 January 1966. Badly damaged in collision with Japanese cargo ship
TOKAI MARU in Irako Strait, 27 November 1971.

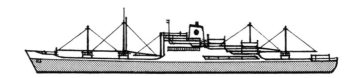

215 ORIENTAL INVENTOR

'55, (1967-   ) 8,245. 538 x 64. Single screw, motorship, 16 knots. 86 passengers. Built by Bremer
Vulkan, Vegesack as HANNOVER for Hamburg American Line (West Germany). Route: Hamburg-
Far East. Bought by Orient Overseas Line 1966; renamed ORIENTAL INVENTOR. F.V. New
York-West Coast and Orient, January 1967. Route: Hong Kong, Taiwan, Japan-Los Angeles, Gulf
and East Coast ports of United States.

216 ORIENTAL HERO

'54, (1967-   ) 8,244. Details as (215). Built by Bremer Vulkan as FRANKFURT for Hamburg
American Line. Bought by Orient Overseas Line 1966; renamed ORIENTAL HERO. F.V. February
1967. Collided with, and sank Greek freighter CASTOR in North Pacific, 28 June 1971.

217 ORIENTAL LADY

'55, (1967-   ) 8,270. Details as (215). Built by Bremer Vulkan as BAYERNSTEIN for Norddeutscher Lloyd (West Germany). Bought by Orient Overseas Line 1967; renamed ORIENTAL LADY.
F.V. March 1967.

218 ORIENTAL MUSICIAN

'54, (1968-) 8,213. Details as (215). Built by Bremer Vulkan as HESSENSTEIN for Norddeutscher Lloyd. Bought by Orient Overseas Line 1967; renamed ORIENTAL MUSICIAN. F.V. April 1967.

219 ORIENTAL WARRIOR

'54, (1967-72) 8,269. Details as (215). Built by Bremer Vulkan as HAMBURG for Hamburg American Line. Bought by Orient Overseas Line 1967; renamed ORIENTAL WARRIOR. F.V. May 1967. Abandoned by passengers and crew 30 miles off Florida coast, 25 May 1972 after fire broke out in engine room. Towed to Jacksonville two days later, where she stttled on bottom. Refloated, towed to sea and scuttled, 1 October 1972

220 ORIENTAL RULER

'54, (1967-) 8,269. Details as (215). Built by Bremer Vulkan as SCHWABENSTEIN for Norddeutscher Lloyd. Bought by Orient Overseas Line 1967; renamed ORIENTAL RULER. F.V. June 1967.

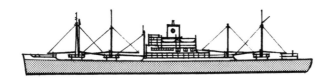

221 ORIENTAL AMIGA

'50, (1968-) 10,150. 498 x 69. Single screw, turbines, 16.5 knots. 60 passengers. Built by Wilton-Fijenoord, Schiedam as DIEMERDYK for Holland-America Line (Netherlands). M.V. Rotterdam-New York, June 1950. Route: Northern Europe-West Coast of United States. Bought by Orient Overseas Line 1968; renamed ORIENTAL AMIGA. F.V. New York-West Coast and Orient, December 1968. Route: Hong Kong, Keelung-Japanese ports and Los Angeles.

222 ORIENTAL FANTASIA

'57, (1970-) 10,417. 504 x 69. Details as (221). Built by Wilton-Fijenoord as DINTELDYK for Holland-America Line. Bought by Orient Overseas Line 1970; renamed ORIENTAL FANTASIA. F.V. New York-West Coast and Orient, December 1970.

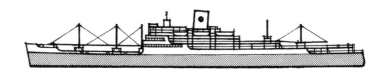

223 ORIENTAL RIO

'51, (1969-) 17,851. Formerly RUAHINE (12) New Zealand Shipping Co. Bought by Orient Overseas Line 1968; renamed ORIENTAL RIO. Registered in Taiwan. Route: Eastbound round-the-world. F.V. from San Diego, 26 February 1969.

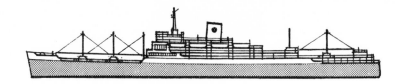

224   ORIENTAL ESMERALDA
'50, (1969-   ) 19,567. Formerly RANGITANE (11) New Zealand Shipping Co. Bought by
Astroguardo Cia Nav (Greece) for breaking up 1968; renamed JAN. Bought by Orient Overseas
Line later in year; renamed ORIENTAL ESMERALDA. Route: Eastbound round-the-world
F.V. from San Diego, 4 June 1969.

225   ORIENTAL CARNAVAL
'50, (1970-   ) 16,661. Formerly RANGITOTO (10) New Zealand Shipping Co. Bought by Orient
Overseas Line 1969; renamed ORIENTAL CARNAVAL. Route: Eastbound round-the-world. F.V.
from San Diego, April 1970.

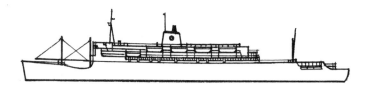

226   UNIVERSE CAMPUS
'53, (1971-   ) 13,950. 564 x 76. Single screw, turbines, 20 knots. Built by Sun Shipbuilding &
Dry Dock Co, Chester, Pa as cargo liner BADGER MARINER. Bought by American Banner Line
(United States) 1957; renamed ATLANTIC and refitted as passenger ship. F.V. New York-
Amsterdam, 11 June 1958. Bought by American Export Lines (United States) 1959 for New York-
Mediterranean service; laid up at Baltimore March 1968. Bought by Orient Overseas Line 1971;
renamed UNIVERSE CAMPUS. Refitted as floating campus for Chapman College, Orange, Calif
F.V. Los Angeles-round-the-world, 3 September 1971.

SHIPS NOT ILLUSTRATED

GREAT BRITAIN

Eastern & Australian Steamship Co

227   ST ALBANS
'10, (1910-31) 4,119. 367 (R) x 47. Single screw, triple expansion engine, 14 knots. Built by Workman, Clark & Co, Belfast. M.V. Barry-Shanghai, Kobe, Sydney and Melbourne, 21 July 1910. Route: Australia-Manila, Hong Kong and Japan. Broken up Yokohama 1931.

228   ARAFURA
'03, (1920-9) 5,597. 403 (R) x 49. Single screw, triple expansion engine, 11 knots. Built by Bremer Vulkan, Vegesack as cargo ship FLORIDA for Argo Line (Germany). Bought by Woermann Line (Germany) 1904; renamed PROFESSOR WOERMANN. Bought by Hamburg American Line (Germany) 1907; renamed SWAKOPMUND. Ceded to British Government as war reparation 1919. Assigned to Eastern & Australian Steamship Co 1920; renamed ARAFURA. Accommodation provided for 30 saloon passengers. Sold to Osaka Shosen Kaisha 1929; broken up Osaka 1930.

Australian Oriental Line,   Hong Kong

229   CHANGTE
'25, (1925-61) 4,324. 368 x 48. Single screw, triple expansion engine, 12 knots. 91 passengers. Built by Hong Kong & Whampoa Dock Co, Kowloon. Route: Japan-Hong Kong, Manila and Australia. Broken up Hong Kong 1961.

230   TAIPING
'26, (1926-61) 4,324. Details as (229). Built by Hong Kong & Whampoa Dock Co. Broken up Hong Kong 1961.

Pacific Shipowners,   Suva

231   LEVUKA
'45, (1947-8), 7,461. 440 x 57. Single screw, triple expansion engine, 12 knots. Built by West Coast Shipbuilders, Vancouver as Royal Navy landing craft maintenance ship HMS DUNGENESS. Bought by Pacific Shipowners 1947; renamed LEVUKA. Refitted with accommodation for 60 passengers. Route: Vancouver-Honolulu, Fiji and Sydney. Sold to British Phosphate Commissioners 1948; renamed TRIADIC.

232   LAKEMBA
'45, (1947-67) 7,459. Details as (231). Built by Burrard Dry Dock Co, North Vancouver as HMS SPURN POINT. Bought by Pacific Shipowners 1947; renamed LAKEMBA. Refitted with accommodation for 98 passengers. Grounded on reef off Vatulele, Fiji and abandoned 5 October 1967. Sank in deep water four days later.

Indo-China Steam Navigation Co,   Hong Kong

233   EASTERN QUEEN
'50, (1950-70) 8,644. 468 x 63. Single screw, turbines, 15 knots. Built by Wm Denny & Bros, Dumbarton. 26 First Class passengers plus several hundred steerage and deck passengers. Route: Japan-Hong Kong, Australia. Sold to Wicklow Shipping Co (Gibraltar) 1970; renamed WICKLOW.

UNITED STATES

Matson Lines

234 LURLINE
'08, (1908-28) 6,572. 437 x 53. Single screw, triple expansion engine, 13.5 knots. 51 passengers. Built by Newport News Shipbuilding & Drydock Co, Newport News,Va F.V. San Francisco-Honolulu, 6 June 1908. Transferred to San Francisco, Seattle-Honolulu service 1922. Sold to Alaska Packers Assoc (United States) 1928; renamed CHIRIKOF. Sold to Jugolinija (Yugoslavia) 1947; renamed RADNIK. Broken up 1952.

235 MANOA
'13, (1914-43) 6,806. 422 (R) x 54. Single screw, quadruple expansion engine, 14 knots. Built by Newport News SB & DD Co F.V. SanFrancisco-Honolulu, 17 March 1914. Ceased carrying passengers 1932. Sold to Soviet Union 1943; renamed BALHASH.

States Steamship Co,   Portland

236 GENERAL LEE
'08, (1933-8) 4,732. 379 (R) x 50. Single screw, triple expansion engine, 13 knots. 103 passengers. Built by Workman, Clark & Co, Belfast as CARTAGO for United Fruit Steamship Co. Registered in Great Britain; registry transferred to United States 1914. Chartered by States Steamship Co 1932; renamed GENERAL LEE. Route: Portland, San Francisco-Far East. Reverted to United Fruit Co 1938; renamed CARTAGO. Broken up Tampa, Florida 1949.

237 GENERAL PERSHING
'08, (1933-8) 4,732. Details as (236). Built by Workman, Clark & Co as HEREDIA for United Fruit. Chartered by States Steamship Co 1932; renamed GENERAL PERSHING. Reverted to United Fruit 1938; renamed HEREDIA. Torpedoed and sunk in Gulf of Mexico, 19 May 1942.

238 GENERAL SHERMAN
'08, (1933-8) 4,611. Details as (236). Built by Workman, Clark & Co as PARISMINA for United Fruit. Chartered by States Steamship Co 1932; renamed GENERAL SHERMAN. Reverted to United Fruit 1938; renamed PARISMINA. Torpedoed and sunk, 18 November 1942.

JAPAN

Nippon Yusen Kaisha

239 TANGO MARU
'05, (1910-30) 6,893. 456 (R) x 50. Twin screw, triple expansion engines, 14 knots. Built by Mitsubishi Dockyard; the largest ship built in Japanese yards up to that time. Route: Japan-Europe via Suez Canal. Transferred to Australia service 1910. Diverted to wartime service 1917-22; transferred to Bombay service 1930. Sunk by American aircraft in East China Sea, 13 November 1943.

240 YOKOHAMA MARU
'12, (1912-33) 6,143. 409 (R) x 49. Twin screw, triple expansion engines, 14 knots. Built by Mitsubishi Dockyard; delivered 14 May 1912. Route: Japan-Seattle. Transferred to South Seas service 1933. Sunk by American aircraft 10 March 1942.

241 SHIDZUOKA MARU
'12, (1912-33) 6,469. Details as (240). Built by Kawasaki Dockyard, Kobe; delivered 24 June 1912.
Route: Seattle service. Ran aground 23 April 1933 and abandoned as total loss three weeks later.

242 ANYO MARU
'13, (1913-30) 9,257. 466 (R) x 58. Twin screw, turbines, 13 knots. Built by Mitsubishi Dockyard
for Toyo Kisen Kaisha; delivered June 1913. Route: Japan-West Coast of South America. Transferred to NYK Line 1926; F.V. Yokohama-Hong Kong, South American ports, 21 March 1926.
Laid up October 1930; sailed on Bombay service 1932. Sold to Nanyo Kaiun Kaisha February 1943.
Torpedoed and sunk by USS BARB in Formosa Strait, 8 January 1945.

243 RAKUYO MARU
'21, (1921-43) 9,419. 460 (R) x 60. Details as (242). Built by Mitsubishi Dockyard for Toyo Kisen
Kaisha; delivered May 1921. Route: Japan-West Coast of South America. Transferred to NYK Line
1926; F.V. Yokohama-Hong Kong, South America, 19 June 1926. Sold to Nanyo Kaiun Kaisha
1943. Torpedoed and sunk by USS SEALION II in Tonkin Gulf, 12 September 1944.

Osaka Shosen Kaisha

244 TACOMA MARU
'09, (1909-44) 5,772. 420 (R) x 50. Twin screw, triple expansion engines, 13 knots. Built by
Kawasaki Dockyard, Kobe; delivered 25 May 1909. Route: Japan-Seattle, Vancouver, Victoria
and Tacoma; transferred to South American service June 1917-December 1923. Torpedoed and
sunk by USS HAKE off Halmahera, 1 February 1944.

245 SEATTLE MARU
'09, (1909-44) 5,853. Details as (244). Built by Kawasaki Dockyard; delivered 26 July 1909.
Route: Japan-Tacoma; transferred to South America service June 1917-August 1925. Torpedoed
and sunk by USS PIRANHA in Sulu Sea, 16 July 1944.

246 CHICAGO MARU
'10, (1910-43) 5,853. Details as (244). Built by Kawasaki Dockyard; delivered 12 January 1910.
Route: Japan-Tacoma; transferred to South America service February 1920-August 1926.
Torpedoed and sunk by USS TULLIBEE in Formosa Strait, 15 October 1943.

247 MEXICO MARU
'10, (1910-44) 5,785. 408 (R) x 50. Twin screw, triple expansion engines, 13 knots. Built by
Mitsubishi Dockyard, Nagasaki; delivered 12 October 1910. Route: Japan-Tacoma; transferred to
South America service February 1920-August 1926. Torpedoed and sunk by USS JACK in Celebes
Sea, 29 August 1944.

248 PANAMA MARU
'10, (1910-35) 5,806. Details as (247). Built by Mitsubishi Dockyard; delivered January 1910.
Route: Japan-Tacoma; transferred to South America service June 1917-August 1925. Broken up
1935.

249 CANADA MARU
'11, (1911-35) 5,780. Details as (247). Built by Mitsubishi Dockyard; delivered January 1911.
Route: Japan-Tacoma; transferred to South America service February 1920-May 1926. Broken up
1935.

Toyo Yusen Kaisha

250   ORIENTAL QUEEN

'36, (1961-   ) 11,004. Formerly KANIMBLA (81) McIlwraith, McEacharn Ltd. Bought by
Pacific Transit Co (Panama) 1961; renamed ORIENTAL QUEEN. Operated in pilgrim trade.
Chartered by Toyo Yusen Kaisha for Japan-Australia service 1964. Purchased 1967; registry
transferred to Japan.

APPENDIX

THE TWENTY LARGEST PACIFIC LINERS IN ORDER OF OVERALL LENGTH

		NAME	YEAR	LINE	O.L.	G.R.T.
*	1	CANBERRA	1961	P & O LINES	818	44,807
*	2	ORIANA	1961	ORIENT LINE	804	41,910
*	3	AUSTRALIS	1940	CHANDRIS LINES	723	34,449
*	4	ORSOVA	1954	ORIENT LINE	723	29,091
*	5	ARCADIA	1954	P & O LINES	721	29,871
*	6	IBERIA	1948	P & O LINES	719	29,779
*	7	ORCADES	1948	ORIENT LINE	709	28,472
*	8	ORONSAY	1951	ORIENT LINE	709	28,136
*	9	HIMALAYA	1949	P & O LINES	709	28,047
*	10	GUGLIELMO MARCONI	1963	LLOYD TRIESTINO	702	27,905
*	11	GALILEO GALILEI	1963	LLOYD TRIESTINO	702	27,888
*	12	CHUSAN	1950	P & O LINES	673	24,318
*	13	ANGELINA LAURO	1939	FLOTTA LAURO	672	24,377
	14	EMPRESS OF JAPAN	1930	CANADIAN PACIFIC	666	26,313
	15	ORION	1935	ORIENT LINE	665	23,696
	16	PRESIDENT HOOVER	1931	DOLLAR LINE	654	21,936
	17	PRESIDENT COOLIDGE	1931	DOLLAR LINE	654	21,936
	18	EMPRESS OF CANADA	1922	CANADIAN PACIFIC	653	21,516
*	19	NORTHERN STAR	1962	SHAW SAVILL LINE	650	23,983
*	20	ELLINIS	1932	CHANDRIS LINES	642	24,251

SHIPS BUILT UNDER ANOTHER NAME

AUSTRALIS	ex	AMERICA	United States Lines
ANGELINA LAURO		ORANJE	Nederland Line
ELLINIS		LURLINE	Matson Lines

* SHIPS IN SERVICE 1972

Note: What would have been by far the largest Pacific liner, the SEAWISE UNIVERSITY '40/83,673. (ex QUEEN ELIZABETH. Cunard Line) operated by Orient Overseas Line and registered in Panama, caught fire and sank in Hong Kong harbour 10 January 1972 shortly before the scheduled completion of her refit as a cruise ship and floating university.

LIST OF SOURCES

Benson, Richard — Steamships and Motorships of the West Coast
Dunn, Laurence — Famous Liners of the Past, Belfast Built
Passenger Liners
Ship Recognition, Liners
A Short History of Japanese Merchant Shipping

Furuta, Ryoichi and Yoshikazu Hirai
Gibbs, C.R. Vernon — British Passenger Liners of the Five Oceans
Isherwood, J.H. — Steamers of the Past
Sea Breezes Famous Ships

Lawson, Will — Pacific Steamers
Maber, John M. — North Star to Southern Cross
Musk, George — Canadian Pacific 1891-1961
Newell, Gordon — Ocean Liners of the Twentieth Century
Smith, Eugene W. — Passenger Ships of the World, Past and Present
Stewart, I.G. — The Ships that Serve New Zealand
Talbot-Booth, E.C. — Merchant Ships
Waters, Sydney D. — Union Line
Shaw Savill Line

Williams, Peter — Ships in Australian Waters
Worker, Colin F. — The World's Passenger Ships

Golden Jubilee History of Nippon Yusen Kaisha 1885-1935

Periodicals

Fairplay International Shipping Journal
Marine News
Merchant Ships, World Built
The Motor Ship
Sea Breezes

INDEX OF SHIPS